Psilocybin Mushrooms

The Complete Step-by-Step Guide to Growing and Using Psychedelic Magic Mushrooms and Discover Benefits and Side Effects
(2022 Edition for Beginners)

Harlan Dean

MUSHROOM CULTIVATION:
A BEGINNER'S GUIDE

TABLE OF CONTENT

A budget-friendly option
Cultivation process steps
Culture media examples
The making of psilocybin mushrooms
Seed or inocula
Mushroom cultivation
Handling after the harvest
Composting mushrooms
Phase 2: completion of the compost 20
Outdoor air will take its place.
Spawning
Spawning supplementation
Various types
Inoculus's residence
Supplement for the fall
Mounting
Cultivation
Mushroom harvesting
Pasteurization
Sowing
Pasteurized straw cooling
Substrates
Nutrients for cultivation recommendations
Vitamin d is an important nutrient.
Fiber in food (df)
Selenium
Potassium
Antioxidants

Conditions in the environment
Mushroom post-crop compost disposal
Grow champis on your own
Psilocybin mushrooms grown on tree trunks

The best psilocybin mushroom growing wood
Which mushrooms are there?
Mushroom with oysters (pleurotus ostreatus)
Samtfubrübling / enoki (flammulina elutipes)

Gathering food from the wild
Equipment is required.
Lightly separate the mushrooms from the earth.
How to make the most of your mushrooms
Seeding advice
What are the requirements?
Recommendation at the end

INTRODUCTION

It's worth noting that nutritional truffles are referred to as mushrooms. It can be mixed with plants, but they are not plants because they lack chlorophyll, which is required for photosynthesis, and they require different requirements for optimal growth because their metabolism is similar to that of animals in that it does not allow complex compounds to form due to light. Photosynthesis is a process in which plants convert atmospheric carbon dioxide into carbohydrates, particularly cellulose. While plants acquire their energy from sunlight, mushrooms get all of their energy and growth resources from their means of growth, which are broken down biochemically. When we say fungi, we're talking about mushrooms, and when we say truffle, we're talking about mushrooms as well. The various types can be cultivated in enclosed and dark environments such as tubes or basements, which are ideal because they maintain a comfortable temperature and a high and consistent humidity. However, because some fungi use light as a signal to yield fruit, this does not indicate that light is not required. All of the ingredients required for growth, on the other hand, must already be present in the environment in which it will be generated. Fungi thrive in high moisture environments, such as 95 to 100 percent humidity and 50 to 75 percent humidity on the substrate. Fungi reproduce sexually throughout their underground growth and asexually through spores instead of seeds. Any of these can be infected by an airborne microorganism, which prevents the mushroom from germinating and resulting in a healthy harvest. As you delve more into this book, you will discover what will pique your interest in beginning to cultivate mushrooms, whether outdoors or indoors. You may have heard things about mushrooms that were incorrect in the past, but you will see how magical they are in this book. So, cross your legs and enjoy the ride to being a master mushroom cultivator.

CHAPTER ONE
MUSHROOM CULTIVATION'S HISTORY

The most common mushroom species is Agaricus bisporus, which belongs to the Agaricaceae family. We're talking about white champignons, which come in a variety of colors. The film is set in the early twentieth century in Paris, France, and depicts the use of mushrooms in culinary art. As a result, this dish was dubbed the "mushroom of Paris" at first. This fungus is being consumed all around the world. Fungi are found all over the world, and there are around 10,000 different species, only 10% of which are edible. Because edible mushrooms have an average protein level of 19 to 35 percent based on dry weight, compared to 23.8 percent in chicken, 19.4 percent in beef, and 25.2 percent in milk, protein is considered the most important nutritional feature. In rural places, it is a viable alternative to food subsistence. It is founded on the concept of utilizing agricultural by-products. It is an easy-to-implement technology that can be used as a secondary source of revenue. Psilocybin is the most popular mushroom species. The usage of mushrooms in culinary art is set in the early twentieth century in Paris, France, and we discuss the magical mushroom, which has several kinds. As a result, this dish was dubbed the "mushroom of Paris" at first. This fungus is being consumed all around the world. Psilocybin mushrooms are inherently hallucinogenic and have been used for spiritual and ceremonial purposes by humans for thousands of years. They belong to the mushroom family, as their name implies. They are distinct because they do not belong to the animal kingdom or the plant kingdom; they are a separate life form. Fungi have DNA that is more similar to that of animals than it is to that of plants. The presence of psychoactive components, such as psilocybin, distinguishes this species of fungus. Psilocybin is one of nature's most powerful hallucinogenic chemicals. It affects the central nervous system, which alters a person's perspective of reality and behavior. A person's senses become more distorted and acute after ingesting a large amount of Psilocybin. Colors appear to be more bright, sounds appear to be more strong, and even touch appears to have been altered. Psilocybin has the ability to alter a person's emotions and state of mind, causing them to feel a sense of awe and thankfulness. After taking psilocybin mushrooms, many people claim mystical and religious experiences, as well as long-term positive effects on their attitude on life. It's been dubbed "the meal of the gods" by anthropologist and psychonaut Terrence McKenna, and it's been outlawed in many nations for a long time. Some researchers, on the other hand, have obtained access to these chemicals in order to study their effects on the human brain. Although research is currently ongoing, and the majority of it is prohibited, promising results have emerged in the treatment of a variety of mental diseases. At certain periods of the year, psilocybin mushrooms can be found growing in various countries throughout the world. In other places, the season might be shortened, and those caught red-handed gathering these interesting mushrooms in the fields may face legal consequences. However, there is another way to obtain these mushrooms, and that is to cultivate them at home in the safety and security of your own house. Only a few components and the proper technique are required. Plants and animals were separated into two major categories at some point in history. Fungi were first classified as plants because they had a cell wall, which is also present in plants but missing in mammals. However, this classification is incorrect because the fungi lack chlorophyll, making photosynthesis impossible for them. Fungi are heterotrophic creatures, which means they must change organic substances obtained through their cell walls through an absorption process in order to feed. Fungi have features that set them apart from plants and animals, thus they've been given their own kingdom, Fungi. Fungi have been utilized by humans since ancient times; the Greeks believed that they provided strength to warriors, while the Egyptian pharaohs admired them for their delicacy. They were regarded "food of the gods" by the Romans and were only eaten on special occasions; the Chinese named them "the elixir of life" since they were considered a healthful diet. Indigenous Mexicans, for their part, have utilized them as hallucinogens in religious ceremonies and for therapeutic purposes since pre-Hispanic times. The cultivation and manufacture of some wild mushrooms under controlled conditions stretches back more than 2,000 years; the first mushroom is thought to have been cultivated in China around

600 BC. In Mexico, mushroom production began in 1933 with the cultivation of Agaricus bisporus (mushroom), followed by the advancement of Pleurotus ostreatus (mushroom) in 1974 and Pleurotus ostreatus (mushroom) in 1984. The present national production of grown mushrooms is expected to be just over 55 thousand tons, an increase of more than 100% over the volume produced 13 years ago. More than 85% of the production goes to mushrooms, 10% to mushrooms, and 0.1 percent to shiitake mushrooms. Fungi cultivation has taken place in two ways in our country: private industrial production and agricultural production, the latter of which began about 25 years ago. The application of farming techniques at the provincial level has been a priority over the last two decades. Due to the simplicity of cultivation and low initial investment, some research centers, such as the Institute of Ecology, have implemented a technology transfer model with the possibility of incorporating these techniques into rural development and leading to a large number of small producers, primarily mushrooms. This type of approach has generally allowed them to be incorporated as a family's additional activity; on the one hand, they receive a part of food with high nutritional content, and on the other, they gain financially.

A Budget-Friendly Option

When agriculture becomes less stable due to climate change, mushroom growing might be a good source of income. It can also be used as a backup power source for the household. Fungi are high in protein, vitamins, and minerals and grow quickly. It is a great hobby for both rural and urban regions because it does not require land to cultivate them. Mushrooms can be grown in a variety of ways. They can be grown in plastic bags, pots, logs, or stacked wooden trays, or anywhere where the intensity of light, temperature, and water can be managed. It is feasible to control the conditions for cultivation using a simple structure. The crop cycle might span anywhere from one to three months. Before you begin cultivating them, if possible, seek advice from someone with sufficient experience. Various edible fungus species have adapted to various culture mediums. Some species, on the other hand, may be cultivated in a variety of materials. Rice straw, rice bran, banana leaves, sawdust, and logs can all be used to make the culture media (see box). In tropical climates, the most common mushroom species include girobola, Volvariella, and maitake. Select a culture medium that is simple to get. It should be cut, then soaked in water for several days to kill insects before being dried and mixed with lime and fertilizer. It should be disinfected with steam if possible. A sterilizer can be made from a 200-liter container or something similar. Adapt the box so that the culture medium can be placed on top and water can be brought to a boil at the bottom. Then, add the fungal spores to the growth media in containers. Keep in mind that fungal spores are best created in sterile environments. It's possible that you'll have to purchase the spores from a specialized supplier. You can look for local providers on the Internet or by inquiring around your neighborhood, universities, or non-profit organizations. After they've been placed in the culture medium, the spores will generate mycelia, which looks like white strands and takes ten days to expand in the culture medium. Mycelia will start producing fungus, which will grow in batches every number of days. After two or three months, when mushroom production begins to decline, the process can be restarted. Make use of the culture medium as fertilizer or compost for other crops.

Cultivation Process Steps

1. Identify and clean a location or containers where temperature, light intensity, and humidity may be adjusted.

2. Choose a culture media and prepare it.

3. Make sure the culture media is clean.

4. Disperse the spores in the culture medium's bags or beds.

5. Set the proper temperature, humidity, hygiene, and light levels. These variables differ depending on the species.

6. Mushrooms are harvested, processed, gathered, and sold.

7. Rinse out the growth area and start over with fresh culture medium and spores. Fungi are sensitive organisms. Catch them with a sharp knife and transfer them to baskets or boxes. If you have any leftover mushrooms, you can dry them and preserve them for later use. Ideally, buy new spores every time the procedure starts. If this is difficult or expensive, you can use a portion of the culture medium from earlier crops, as well as the spores found in it, for the new culture medium.

Culture Media Examples

Rice or wheat straw is appropriate for girobola, rice, and grassland mushrooms. Coffee pulp is a good match for shiitake and girobola mushrooms. Sawdust is appropriate for shiitake, girobola, lion mane, Judas ear, and maitake mushrooms. Mushroom rice and mushroom girobola go well with water hyacinth. In Mexico, the fungi of the genus Pleurotus are referred to as "mushrooms," but they are also known as white ears, stick ears, satan can ears, peanut ears, and some ears. Given the state of Veracruz's geographic location, climate, and abundance of agricultural waste (stubble of various straws) and agro-industrial waste (coffee pulp and sugarcane bagasse), mushroom cultivation appears to be a viable alternative for the use of this waste and the production of a nutritious edible product (fungi). Because of its ability to grow on a variety of substrates and develop over a wide temperature range, this fungus is a viable social and economic option in the state's central region. Characteristics in General

Mushrooms can be found growing naturally in decaying logs or various agricultural products. As a result, agroindustrial wastes can be used to construct them. Because they feed on the organic matter in which they develop, it is critical to provide a proper substrate for the fungus when trying to cultivate it so that it may absorb the nutrients. Mushrooms also require a consistent temperature and humidity, as well as oxygen-rich air and a specific amount of light. These fungi are regarded as a dietary supplement with acceptable nutritional value. All of the necessary amino acids are present in its proteins. On a dry weight basis, it contains between 57 and 61 percent carbs, 26 percent protein, and 11.9 percent fiber; it is also low in fat. Vitamins like niacin, thiamine, B12, and C are all good for you. Potassium, phosphorus, and calcium, among other minerals, are all present. Mushrooms also contain anticancer polysaccharides as well as erythedenine, a substance licensed by the FDA (Food and Drug Administration) in 1987 to treat high blood cholesterol levels in the United States.

The Making of Psilocybin Mushrooms

The generation of the seed or inoculum, the production of fresh mushrooms, and postharvest management are the three operations involved in this technology.

Seed or inocula

The manufacture of inoculum, which refers to the propagation of huge fungus development in grasses grains, is the foundation for commercial mushroom cultivation. This inoculum is spread on the substrate (sowing), where the fungus (fruiting) will grow. The inoculum is one of the most difficult issues for commercial Psilocybin mushroom growers because its preparation necessitates the use of a microbiological laboratory and a highly skilled technician, implying a higher initial and ongoing expenditure in installation and maintenance. The inoculum can be purchased from a specific provider or research institution, and the quality of the inoculum has a direct impact on the availability of fresh mushrooms.

Mushroom cultivation

It starts with the creation or customization of a room that meets the fungus's environmental conditions and requirements. The substrate is exposed to a heat treatment technique (pasteurization) for Psilocybin mushroom growing to eliminate dangerous bacteria present in the substrate; pasteurization can be done by steam injection or immersion in hot water. After that, the substrate is placed in plastic bags and inoculum is sown on it (seed). The bags containing the infected substrate are incubated for two to three weeks in the dark (23-27 ° C). Fungi are obtained 25 to 30 days after planting, under ideal lighting, ventilation, and humidity conditions (75-90 percent).

Handling After the Harvest

The fungi are consumed shortly after harvesting, sold fresh, or kept refrigerated (2-3 °C). To avoid abuse, its commercialization is done in bulk or packaging, which lowers the quality and hence the cost. Small trays coated in transparent plastic film, cardboard boxes, or plastic baskets are examples of packing. Fungi lose 1 to 2% of their initial weight per day, thus commercialization must happen quickly. The mushroom is presented at the point of sale, mostly fresh in bulk and in smaller quantities. The Mushroom

Cultivation Unit is located within the Institute of Ecology AC (INECOL). It does research on the biotechnology of a few edible fungus species. In addition to research, it is responsible for giving courses and training workshops to professionals and university students who are interested in learning about the process of psilocybin mushroom production. A laboratory for experimentation and seed production, incubation rooms, a mushroom planting room, production areas for fresh mushrooms with controlled air circulation, irrigation, and temperature, a cold room, and a zone for drying and postharvest fungus treatment are among the areas in which the environmental parameters that favor the development of fungi are automatically controlled. This Unit is currently a core from which fruitful projects, training, and specialty training emanate, not only in Mexico but also throughout Latin America. If you're interested in learning the fundamentals of psilocybin mushroom farming, sign up for the Workshop-Workshop "Theoretical and technical principles of edible mushroom cultivation (Pleurotus)," which has the following goals: The purpose of this paper is to present the scientific, theoretical, and practical foundations of mushroom growing. To provide information about production control equipment and systems. To give attendees with information that will assist them in creating a production strategy that is tailored to their specific needs and capabilities. In addition to supporting proper farming techniques, order, control, and cleaning, which allows for profitable and successful activities. Entrepreneurs, professionals, consultants, teachers, students, and the general public will benefit from it. Over the previous 25 years, many processes in psilocybin mushroom cultivation have been conducted, including the employment of the following techniques: Aeration through force Tunnels spawn run in large numbers Inoculum inoculum inoculum inoculum inoculum in Supplementing with humus Crosses Mushrooms' nutritional status has improved. Alternative post-harvest mushroom composting processes necessitate a reorganized and extended update. The growing of psilocybin mushrooms is divided into six stages, and while the divisions are a little arbitrary, these stages identify what is required to set up a production system. Phase I composting, Phase II composting, spawning, casing, pinning, and cropping are the six levels. These Stages are presented in their natural order, stressing the key characteristics of each Stage. The fertilizer offers the nutrients that fungi require to thrive. There are two types of materials frequently used for mushroom fertilizer, with wheat straw bedded horse manure being the most widely utilized and having the lowest cost rate. Synthetic fertilizer is commonly created from grass and grain silage, although the term is used to describe any mushroom fertilizer that does not contain animal dung as the primary ingredient. Nitrogen sequels and a conditioning ingredient, gypsum, are required in both types of fertilizers. Phase I and Phase II composting are the two stages in the fertilizer establishment process. Phase I of composting is where the analysis of fertilizer combination and psilocybin mushroom development begins. 1st Phase:

Composting Mushrooms

The first phase was Composting begins with the ingredients being mixed and wet in a rectangle mound with tight sides and a loose middle. The bulk materials are usually dropped through a compost turner. As the horse compost or synthetic fertilizer passes through the turner, water is sprayed on it. The turner scatters nitrogen additions and gypsum across the top of the bulk materials, thoroughly fraternizing them. The pile is wetted and produced right away. The germination and production of microorganisms, which freely transpire in the bulk ingredients, initiates aerobic agitation (composting). As a result of this method, radiation, ammonia, and carbon dioxide are released as by-products. The mushroom business has almost universally adopted high-pressure aeration, in which fertilizer is deposited on a cement floor or in tubes or lockers and aerated by a high-pressure section of ventilation via a plenum, vents, or valves located in the basement. When the chemical nature of raw materials is modified by the activity of microorganisms, heat, and certain chemical processes that produce heat, fungal compost is created. These events result in a more favorable food source for the growth of psilocybin mushrooms, as well as other fungi and bacteria. Unless the method stops, sufficient humidity, oxygen, nitrogen, and carbohydrates must be part of the method today. This is why the fertilizer pile is vented as it passes through the spinner, and water and additives are added on a regular basis. The quality of the raw materials used to make mushroom compost varies greatly, and it is known to have an impact on the compost's performance in terms of mushroom production and yield.

The use of nitrogen fertilizers, plant growth regulators, and fungicides, as well as the geographical origin of wheat straw, variety (winter or spring), and the use of nitrogen fertilizers, plant growth regulators, and fungicides, can all affect the compost's production. Before making compost, keep wheat straw covered to prevent the growth of undesired and potentially hazardous fungi and bacteria. Gypsum is commonly used to reduce fat content in compost. Gypsum binds to straw or hay rather than fills the pores (holes) between the straws, increasing the flocculation of particular compounds in the compost. The second benefit of this phenomena is that air may enter the chimney more freely, which is important for the composting process. Excluding air creates an anaerobic (airless) environment, which produces toxic chemical compounds that limit the selectivity of mushroom compost for psilocybin mushroom growing. Patches of 40 pounds per ton of dry components supplied at the start of the composting process. Corn, soy, peanuts, cotton, and chicken dung are some of the most regularly utilized nitrogen additives today. These additions are designed to raise the nitrogen content of horse dung to 1.5 percent or 1.7 percent in plastic. The dry weight is used to compute both. The addition of ammonium nitrate or urea to the compost microflora at the start of the composting process to offer a source of nitrogen that is quickly available for growth and reproduction. The initial compost heap should be 5 to 6 feet wide, 5 to 6 feet tall, and take the appropriate amount of time. Although certain turners are fitted with a "ricker," which eliminates the need for a table, a two-sided box can be used to make the stack (rick). The collection's sides should be solid and dense, but the medium should remain free during Phase I composting. The materials become less rigid when the straw or hay softens during composting, and compaction might occur. Quickly. When the content in a traditional Phase I process gets too compact, air cannot flow down the chimney, resulting in an anaerobic atmosphere. Forced ventilation helped to overcome the problem of an anaerobic center core in the compost. Turning and watering should be done every 2-3 days, but only when the battery is heated (145 ° to 170 ° F). The feed allows you to aerate, aerate, mix, and shift straw or hay from one region of a pile to another, both outdoors and inside. When the compost is returned, additions are also added, but they must be added at the start of the composting process. The number of chips and the time between them is determined by the beginning material's characteristics as well as the time it takes for the compost to reach temperatures above 145 degrees Fahrenheit. The addition of water is critical because when bacteria and fungi occupy the area of the pores, too much oxygen is excluded, and just a small amount of oxygen can limit the growth of bacteria and fungi. In general, little or no water is supplied while washing the heap after it has been produced, during the first round, and subsequently during the composting process. Water can be sprayed liberally in the final series before Phase II composting so that the water drains when the compost is securely squeezed. Water, nutritional value, microbial activity, and temperature all have a connection. The entire chain is no longer functional since a condition limits a factor. Phase I of composting takes 6 to 14 days, depending on the type of material used at the start and the qualities of the material for each shift. During composting, a strong ammonia odor can be detected, which is frequently accompanied by a faint mold odor. Chemical changes occur when compost temperatures above 155° F and ammonia is present, resulting in a portion of the food being used exclusively for fungi. The heat emitted and the compost temperatures rise as a result of chemical alterations. When the compost reaches the necessary degree of biological and chemical activity in the second and third rounds, temperatures can reach 170-180 ° F. The compost must have the following characteristics at the end of Phase I: a) a chocolate brown hue b) soft and flexible straws c) Has a moisture content of 68 to 7% d) Has a strong ammonia odor Composting is finished when the specified values for air humidity, temperature, color, and odor are achieved.

PHASE 2: COMPLETION OF THE COMPOST

Pasteurization is required to eliminate insects, nematodes, dangerous fungus, and other parasites that may be present in the compost during Phase II composting. Second, it's critical to condition the compost and remove the ammonia that accumulated during phase I composting. At the end of Phase II, ammonia concentrations greater than 0.07 percent generally hinder fungal brood formation, therefore it must be removed; in general, a person can smell ammonia at concentrations greater than 0.1 percent. Phase II might take one of three forms, depending on the type of production system used. The trays are piled six to eight times and placed in a controlled phase II room in the zone culture system, where the compost is packaged in wooden trays. The dishes were then moved into separate rooms, each offering an ideal environment for each stage of the psilocybin mushroom growing process. Compost is deposited directly on the beds in the room and used at all phases of collecting when using a bed or shelving system. The bulk technology, which was just introduced, involves depositing the compost in an insulated tube with a perforated bottom and computer-controlled ventilation. It's a piece made specifically for Phase II composting. Sterilization and conditioning of compost for mushroom growing in Phase II tunnel. Filling in front of a closed tube on the left, easy to fill on the right. The compost must be uniformly filled in depth, density, and compression, whether it is in beds, trays, or in bulk. The compost should be thick enough to allow for the interchange of ammonia and carbon dioxide gases.

Outdoor air will take its place.

Phase II composting can be conceived of as a temperature-dependent, controlled biological process that uses air to keep the compost at the optimal temperature for microorganism growth and reproduction. The availability of excellent carbohydrates and nitrogen, with some of the nitrogen in the form of ammonia, is critical for the growth of these thermophilic (heat-loving) organisms. Other organisms do not flourish in the compost on which the fungal mycelium develops because these bacteria create or act as nutrients. In recent years, the completion of Phase II in the tunnels has become more common. In comparison to more expensive production rooms, tunnel composting has the advantage of processing more compost per ft2. Tunnel composting, when combined with a loose spawning path, provides the ease of greater consistency and mechanization. In comparison to compost that stays in the same room, transporting finished compost from the pasteurization tunnel to the serial installation tunnel may increase the danger of pathogen and undesired pest infestation. As a result, tunnel composting may necessitate stricter cleanliness standards than indoor composting. When deciding on the technique and order to follow, it's crucial to keep the Phase II objectives in mind. One of the objectives is to get rid of any unwanted ammonia. The temperature range of 125° to 130° F is most useful for this purpose, as bugs thrive in this temperature range. The second goal of Phase II is to use a pasteurization sequence to kill all parasites present in the compost. Before spawning (sowing), the temperature of the compost should be decreased to around 75 to 80 °F toward the conclusion of Phase II. The nitrogen concentration of the requirements should be 2.0 to 2.4 percent, and the moisture content should be 68 to 7%. In addition, for lucrative mushroom crops, 6 to 8 pounds of dry compost per square foot of bed or tray surface should be present at the end of Phase II. Because it is important to have a material that is as homogeneous as possible, it is critical that the fertilizer and compost temperatures are uniformed during the Phase II process.

Spawning

The fungal gills that line the bottom of a fungus's cap create millions of small pores as it matures. These spores function similarly to a higher plant's seeds. Producers, on the other hand, do not employ fungal spores to "sow" the mushroom combination because they sprout in an unpredictable manner and are thus unreliable. Fortunately, mycelium (thin wire-shaped cells) may be vegetatively grown from germinated spores, allowing egg producers to expand their harvest. To ensure that the fungus mycelium remains pure, specialized structures are required to propagate the mycelium. White is the mycelium that has multiplied vegetatively in many grains, or agar, and commercial psilocybin mushroom manufacturers purchase white from companies that specialize in its production. Eggs are produced by sterilizing a mixture of millet grains, water, and chalk; rye, wheat, and other tiny grains can be used instead of millet. Until about 1940, block sterilized horse dung was used as a growing medium for spawning, and this was known as a block, bricklaying, or manure laying; this generation is no longer employed. The grain and mycelium are stirred three times to four days after the sterilized wheat has added mycelium, at intervals of 14 days of active mycelium growth. The mycelium has colonized the grain right away, and the result is termed deposition. Spawning can be done before a breeder orders spawning because it can be refrigerated for a few months. Spawning is evenly sprinkled over the compost, then thoroughly mixed in. This has been done by hand for years, by distributing spawning over the compost's surface and shaking it with a little rake-like tool. However, in recent years, egg laying has been blended with compost using a specific egg-laying machine that mixes composting and laying eggs with teeth or little finger shaped devices for the bed system. When compost flows along a conveyor belt or falls from a conveyor to a box, it generates a system of containers or lots that are combined with compost. For so many square feet of bed cover, the generation rate given in units or a quarter is acceptable; 1 unit by 5ft square is acceptable. A 2 percent growth rate is beneficial. The balance was often shown as a function of the weight of the deposition relative to the weight of the dry compost.

Spawning Supplementation

Increases in performance were noted in egg-laying, the gut, and later when the compost was supplemented with proteins and lipid-rich components in the early 1960s. When tiny amounts of protein supplements were introduced to the farm compost, yields increased by up to ten percent. The amount of vitamins and similar benefits that could be gained were severely limited due to overheating and the development of competitive mold in compost. With the invention of delayed release supplements for fungal culture, these boundaries have been breached (Carroll and Schisler 1976). By encapsulating micro droplets of vegetable oil beneath a layer of denatured protein in formaldehyde, the drawbacks associated with the integration of non-composted nutrients in the fungus compost during placement are mostly eliminated. An increase of up to 60% was achieved. There are various commercial supplements available now that can be utilized to lay eggs or boost fungal performance in the intestine. Manufacturers may be able to boost the performance capacity of their Phase II compost by switching to Micromax as a fungal substrate. Micromax is made up of a blend of nine micronutrients, including (in order of dry weight percentage):

• Caution (12 percent)

• Magnesium (3 percent)

- a (12 percent)

- A (0.1 percent)

- Cucumber (1 percent)

- Feminine (17 percent)

- Mn is a mineral (2.5 percent)

- Motif (0.05 percent)

- Zinc (1 percent)

- Ingredients that are inert (57.35 percent) Mn is responsible for around 70% of the apparent increase in performance, according to research. After the seed and supplement were spread throughout the compost and the compost worked to maintain the surface level, the compost temperature was kept at 75-80 ° F and the relative humidity was kept constant. High to prevent the compost or seed surface from drying out. Egg-laying occurs under these conditions, resulting in a thread-shaped mycelium threading through the compost. From a reproductive grain, mycelium spreads in all directions until the mycelium of the different reproducing granules is merged, changing a biological entity into a fertilizer bed. After fusion, spawning appears as a white to blue-white mass throughout the compost. The seed generates heat as it grows, and if the compost temperature increases over 80° to 85° F, depending on the crop, the weather can kill or harm the mycelium, preventing optimal crop productivity and fungus quality. The growth of the deposit has decreased and the period between deposition and collection has increased at temperatures below 74 ° F.

Phase III and Phase IV are made up of the following components.

When it is retrieved from the borehole and supplied to the producer, phase III compost is a phase II compost that is processed in bulk in a tunnel and can be coated. Phase IV compost is created when phase III compost is caught and the oviposition is able to colonize the coating layer before it is supplied to the culture unit or delivered to the growers. The quality of Phase I and II compounds has a significant impact on the success of Phase III and IV studies. The usage of phase III compost can increase the fungus' quality by fragmenting the colonized compost, which improves the fungus' initial color and shelf life. As the amount of harvest that a producer can expect from their production halls increases, phase III compost has become more popular in recent years. Phase II on-the-shelf production allows for an average of 4.1 plants per year, whereas Phase III bulk fertilizer manufacturing allows for an average of 7.1 plants per year. It's feasible that the number of cultures will grow even more.

Various Types

Mushroom growers in the United States employ three varieties of mushrooms: a) Smooth white hybrids - single cap, cap, and white stem b) Cream hybrid - scaly hat with white stem and cap c) Brown - chocolate brown hood with white bud Each of the three main groupings has many isolates, allowing a grower to choose up to eight cultivars from each. White and whitish hybrids are commonly used in processed meals like soups and sauces, although all isolates are delicious when eaten fresh. Brown variants have gained popularity among consumers in recent years. The crimini kind is comparable to white truffles, but it is browner and has a more rich and earthy flavor. The Portobello mushroom is a huge, brown, open mushroom with crowns up to 6 inches in diameter.

Portobello mushrooms have a meaty texture and a deep scent. The amount of time it takes for spawn to colonize the compost is determined by the pace of deposition and distribution, the compost's moisture and temperature, the compost's integration, and the type or quality of the compost. Typically, the full spawning process takes 13 to 20 days. The next level of production is within reach once the fertilizer with spawning is fully created.

Housing The packaging is placed as a top dressing to the generation compost, which is where the fungi eventually form. As a cover, a mixture of peat and ground limestone might be utilized. The carcass does not require nutrients because it serves as a water reservoir and a breeding ground for rhizomorphs. When the very fine mycelium melts, rhizomorphs resemble thick threads. Rhizomorphs produce mushroom, primordium, or pencil initials. There are no fungi without rhizomorphs. Because humidity is required for the growth of a solid fungus, the shell must be humidity resistant. The roof's primary purpose is to provide water to the mycelium for growth and development, to keep the compost from drying out, to promote fungus development, and to resist structural degradation after watering. The initial source of water to the house that does not pass through the underlying compost has great performance potential. The most common roofing material is peat moss. Brown (new peat, less degraded, slightly structured, superficial) to black (compact, more decomposed, deeply excavated) sphagnum moss can be treated differently at the collecting site. Wet peat is transported in a saturated state, while ground peat is partially dried before packaging and shipment. Because damp peat has a higher water holding capacity than ground peat, some farmers prefer it. Pasteurization is not required because peat shells are free of diseases, weeds, and nematodes, all of which can diminish fungal output. When a 6 cubic foot bale is mixed with 40 pounds of limestone and water, it covers about 125 square feet of compost area at a depth of 2 inches.

Inoculus's Residence

The inoculum coating is a sterilized mixture of peat, vermiculite, and wheat bran that is packed with mycelium from fungi. It is combined with the bale to shorten the harvesting cycle, increase the consistency of mushroom distribution in the bed, and improve the cleanliness of the mushrooms. Because it dissolves in the mycelium of the compost below, Mycelium IC colonizes the covering layer. It enables either several crop interruptions or multiple crops per year. Envelope inoculum promotes mycelial colonization more quickly.

Supplement for the Fall

In the early 1960s, an attempt was made to provide nutrients to the dwellings. The findings revealed that there were far more nutrients on the deck than after laying, and that the improved output was almost proportionate to the added value. While yield gains of up to 100% are achievable, tube level integration has its own set of challenges and potential constraints. After the house is done, the compost should be free of mould, nematodes, and weed pathogens. If the nutritional supplement disintegrates before the organisms, they spread in the compost and can proliferate swiftly before the mycelium fungus begins to grow again. The temperature of the compost must be sustained at roughly 75° F for a maximum of 5 days following the introduction for proper crop management, and the relative air humidity must be high. The compost's temperature should then be dropped by roughly 5 degrees Celsius every day until the first little mushrooms (sticks) appear. Prior to the production of mushroom needles, water should be applied intermittently throughout the post-pack period to regulate the moisture level to the field's capacity. He understands when, how, and how much water should be poured into the box. This is a "art form" that distinguishes expert breeders from others who are just starting out.

Mounting

The shape of the rhizomorphs in the shell determines the initials of the mushrooms. The initials are modest, however they might occur as rhizomorph growths. The structure is a pin once it is an initial quadruplet. During the bud phase, the sticks continue to spread and eventually grow into a mushroom. After 18 to 21 days of covering, the mushrooms are ready to harvest. By delivering fresh air into the living room, the carbon dioxide concentration in the ambient air is lowered to 0.08 percent or less, depending on the kind. The carbon dioxide content of the outside air is approximately 0.0 percent. Mushrooms grow and ripen in the shell, which is surrounded by a 2-inch layer of peat that has been neutralized. The "pens" as well as the young mushrooms may be seen. The timing of the fresh air supply is critical and can only be learned through trial and error. It's normally advisable to breathe as little as possible until the mycelium appears on the envelope's surface and the watering ends when the pens' initials are produced. The mycelium will no longer develop through the shell if carbon dioxide is removed too quickly, and the initials of the mushrooms will form beneath the surface of the shell if it is ventilated too quickly. When swallowed, these mushrooms continue to grow through the casing and become filthy. Insufficient humidity can also contribute to the growth of fungi beneath the surface of the home. Fixation is an important phase in the production cycle that influences both the achievable yield and the quality of a culture.

Cultivation

Rinse, rest, and flowering are terminology describing 3 to 5 day harvest intervals that occur many times during the harvest cycle. After a few days, there are no mushrooms left to be harvested. This cycle repeats itself in a regular pattern, and the harvest can continue as long as the fungus ripen. Most psilocybin mushroom growers harvest between 35 and 42 days, while some take up to 150 days. For best results, keep the air temperature between 57 and 62 degrees Fahrenheit while cutting. This temperature range not only encourages fungal development, but it can also lengthen disease and parasite life cycles. Although it may appear weird that pests can harm fungi, crops that do not compete with other species are not grown. Fungal infestations have the potential to destroy an entire crop. Harvest timings are frequently influenced by the severity of pest infestations. These infections and insects can be controlled through pesticide use and cultural practices. However, excluding these housing groups is extremely desirable. The relative humidity in the living room should be sufficient enough to prevent the wrapper from drying out, but not so high that the budding fungus' surfaces become damp or sticky. Water is applied to the housing so that mildew development is not hampered by water stress. This entails watering two or three times per week in business settings. Depending on the dryness of the shell, the planted variety, and the stage of development of fences, buttons, or fungi, each irrigation might contain more or less liters. When most breeders begin growing for the first time, they pour a lot of water and water on the house's surface. This is referred to as a texture loss on the housing's surface. The sealed housing restricts the exchange of gases that are necessary for fungi to grow. Given that 90% of the fungus is water and a gallon of water weighs 8.3 pounds, it is possible to estimate the amount of water that will be added after the first break. When 100 pounds of mushrooms are harvested, 90 pounds of water (11 gallons) is withdrawn from the shell, which must be replenished before the fungus begin to grow during the second break. During the harvest phase, outdoor air is used to regulate air and compost temperatures. The carbon dioxide generated by the growing mycelium is also displaced by the outside air. The higher the mycelial growth, the more carbon dioxide is produced, and the longer the harvest extension, the more fresh air is required during the first two pauses. The volume of clean air produced is also affected by the number of mushrooms growing, the size of the production space, the amount of compost in the living room, and the conditions or composition of the imported fresh air. When it comes to the volume of air required, experience seems to be the greatest guide, but there is a general rule: 0.3 ft / ft2 / hour when the compost is 8 inches thick, and 50% to 100% of this volume should be out of the air. Fungi require ventilation to develop, as well as the ability to manage humidity and temperature. A cool mist or live steam can be used to create fog, as can simply humidifying the walls and floors. The moisture in the living room can be eliminated.

1) Increase the amount of outside air allowed.

2) Introduce drier air

3) Heat the same amount of outdoor air to a higher temperature because a warmer atmosphere retains more humidity and hence lowers relative humidity.

Controlling the temperature in a mushroom room is similar to controlling the temperature in the rest of the house. The heat could come from the hot water circulating via the wall-mounted pipes. A ventilation duct, which is prevalent in freshly constructed psilocybin mushroom farms, can be used to blow hot and forceful air. Depending on the season of the year, a few mushroom farms are set up in limestone caverns where the rock works as a heat and cooling source outdoors. Caverns of any kind aren't always good for mushroom cultivation, and abandoned coal mines have far too many issues to be regarded viable locations for a psilocybin mushroom farm. Limestone caverns also require substantial rehabilitation and upgrading before being fitted for psilocybin mushroom production, with only growing occurring inside the cave and composting occurring on the ground in a pier. Mushrooms are harvested in a 7 to 10-day cycle, though this might vary based on temperature, humidity, harvest, and harvest phase. A fungus growth inhibitor is removed when mature mushrooms are taken, and the next search begins. Mushrooms were often collected while the veil was not too widely stretched. Consumers in North America prefer closed, thin, white, or brown mushrooms (crimes), however some like open coffee (portobello). The length of the veil, not the size of the fungus, determines the ripeness of the psilocybin mushroom. As a result, mature mushrooms are enormous and small, despite the fact that farmers and consumers prefer medium to large mushrooms.

Mushroom Harvesting

Each mushroom is hand-harvested, with the fungus' base cut off and the clean, ripe mushroom placed in a basket.

• Farm-to-farm variations in pick-and-pack processes are common. Freshly picked mushrooms should be kept in the refrigerator between 35 and 45 degrees Fahrenheit. It is critical to allow the mushrooms to "breathe" after harvesting and then store them in a paper bag to lengthen their shelf life. Using an unwaxed bag is superior to using a plastic bag.

• During the growing of psilocybin mushrooms, the issue of lighting frequently arises. Mushrooms do not require light in order to grow; only green plants require light in order to perform photosynthesis. Growing regions, on the other hand, can be illuminated to make harvesting or cultivation easier.

Pasteurization

There are various requirements for this process, including 2-3 hours at 75°C, 5-8 hours at 70°C, and 1 hour at 93°C. Pasteurization is done with household gas burners, firewood, or boilers with steam injection, using a metal Tambo with 200 liters of water filled to 3/4 capacity. Heats up to the point of boiling. Dry straw is placed in a basket and immersed in hot water for one hour (93-100oC). After that, let it drain for 15 to 20 minutes, or until the basket is no longer dripping (humidity approximately 70-80 percent). The sterile straw is emptied and allowed to cool on a properly washed and sterilized table before being planted. It is necessary to sanitize the planting area.

Sowing

The mushroom fungus will be born from the mycelium. Mycelium is usually produced on hydrated cereal grains (mostly wheat and sorghum).

• The seed is a method in which the mycelial is mixed with the substrate.

• Although transparent 70 x 90cm polyethylene bags can be used, smaller farms should utilize 50 x 70 cm or 40 x 60 cm bags. The straw is also claimed to have lower production efficiency since the huge pouch can overheat if the temperature of the incubation location is high. In practice, the type of bag can be determined based on the specific requirements of each location and the results that have been obtained.

Pasteurized Straw Cooling

A completely disinfected dissecting needle is used to pierce the bags every 5 cm. The pasteurized straw is allowed to cool during sowing, preferably by turning it to allow the contained water vapor to escape. Otherwise, it will condense on the straw, causing issues due to excess moisture. The moisture content of the straw must be between 70 and 80 percent before it can be sowed; in reality, the moisture content is tested by squeezing a fist of straw moderately. If drips from a waterfall or a perceptible amount of humidity remain in the hand, the straw contains too much water. In this scenario, you'll have to wait for it to drain before removing it. Because the fungus requires specific porosity spaces to develop, sowing at greater humidity levels than those recommended is not recommended. This enables for adequate CO2 and oxygen exchange for its growth, avoiding the formation of organisms that can live without oxygen and cause substrate rot. The ideal temperature for sowing is between 24 and 25 degrees Celsius (when it is still a little warm). Because the mycelium dies when sowed with heated straw, it is not recommended. When it is sown with cold straw, on the other hand, the growth is slowed.

Substrates

A substrate is a material that provides food for the fungus; commercially available substrates include wheat straw, corn, and coffee pulp; however, tests have also been conducted with dried bean pods, buffelgrass, oak shavings, henequen bagasse, water lily, coconut fiber, corn, and corn, as well as pepper, cinnamon, lemongrass, and cardamom. This is one of the advantages of mushroom farming, which may take advantage of the local agriculture waste. Because with these sizes, the appropriate substrate must be 5 to 15 cm in size. Better outcomes have been achieved. In order to go through the pasteurization procedure later, the substrate must also be homogeneous.

Nutrients for Cultivation Recommendations

Mushrooms are an excellent source of a variety of nutrients. They are a good source of selenium, riboflavin, and copper, and a good source of niacin (vitamin B3), pantothenic acid (vitamin B5), and potassium (containing more than 10% of the recommended daily amount in one serving). Thiamine (vitamin B1), zinc, vitamin B6, proteins, folic acid, fiber, manganese, and magnesium are all abundant in Criminis. On the other hand, mushrooms are low in fat, salt, and calories. According to the FDA, the nutrients in psilocybin mushrooms are 84 g for raw mushrooms. Saturated fats, trans fats, cholesterol, sugar, vitamin A, and calcium are not necessary nutrients found in mushrooms.

Vitamin D is an important nutrient.

Recent research has discovered that when fungus are exposed to UV radiation, their vitamin D2 level increases significantly. A single serving of mushrooms, which were exposed to ultraviolet light only five minutes after harvest, provides nearly 800 percent of the daily necessary quantity of vitamin D2. People who don't eat fish or drink milk may find this to be a practical way to achieve their daily vitamin D requirements.

Fiber in Food (DF)

Polysaccharides such glycans and glycogen, as well as monosaccharides, disaccharides, sugar alcohols, and chitin, are all found in mushrooms. The majority of polysaccharides (chitin and glucans) are structural components of cell walls and are not digested by humans. As a result, they can be classified as fibers. Dietary fiber can aid in the prevention of many ailments that plague affluent societies. The DF content of portobello mushrooms is higher than that of white mushrooms.

Selenium

According to the USDA National Nutrient Database, a serving (3 ounces) of mushroom crimes contains nearly a third of the recommended daily amount for selenium. According to a longitudinal aging research conducted in Baltimore, selenium decreases prostate cancer by more than 60%. Those with the lowest selenium levels in their blood are four to five times more likely to develop prostate cancer than men with the highest selenium levels, and selenium levels decline with age. By adding sodium selenite to the mushroom compost, the selenium content of the mushrooms can be reliably enhanced. This chemical is being added to several commercial food supplement manufacturers' sustained release nutrients for mushroom cultivation.

Potassium

Crimini fungus are a good supply of potassium, which is necessary for blood pressure regulation, maintaining water balance in fats and muscles, and ensuring cell precision. The potassium content of a 3-ounce portobello mushroom is higher than that of a banana or salmon. Efforts to increase the potassium content of fungus have had mixed results.

Antioxidants

Antioxidants are abundant in portobello and crimini mushrooms, which are also strong sources of antioxidants in carrots, green beans, red peppers, and broccoli. These are excellent sources of polyphenols, the principal antioxidants found in vegetables, as well as L-Ergothioneine (ERGO), a strong antioxidant found only in fungi. Crimini mushrooms have more than 15 times the amount of ERGO found in other ERGO-rich foods.

Conditions in the Environment

The growth of psilocybin mushrooms requires a healthy atmosphere. Here are a few helpful hints. Smell Health-related complaints after processing mushroom compost near residential areas are a problem for some psilocybin mushroom farms. The main cause of these complaints is the foul odors related with the formation of fungal compost. The public has become aware of this problem as a result of a mix of suburbanization and increased public awareness of environmental issues. Many steps have been taken by manufacturers to lessen mushroom cultivation's environmental impact, including forced ventilation of Phase I compost in bunkers or tunnels. The issue of bothersome odors, on the other hand, continues to put strain on psilocybin mushroom farmers.

Mushroom Post-Crop Compost Disposal

The living room must be closed after the last rinse of the mushrooms, and the steam pasteurization chamber and this last pasteurization must be arranged so that any parasites existing in the culture or carpentry in the living room have a low chance of infecting the next crop. The material that remains after mushroom harvest is known as post-harvest mushroom compost. It has a wide range of applications and is a valued horticultural product. The suppression of artillery mushrooms in landscaping is one of MC's key goals. Artillery mushrooms create sticky spore masses the size of a pinhead as they spread across the damp mulch terrain. These spores are violently released on light-colored surfaces like the inside of a house or an automobile. Once the spores have dried, it's difficult to get rid of them without leaving an unattractive dark stain on the surface. Artillery is suppressed by incorporating 20-40% MC into the mulch. When a mushroom is harvested, the post-harvest mushroom compost is placed into a truck.

Grow Champis on Your Own

Starting from scratch and acquiring the necessary tools to grow your mushrooms is the most reliable method. It may appear difficult, but it is not. You'll need to gather spore prints or spore syringes containing the ingredient needed to produce the substrate for mycelium to thrive in a container. To prevent pathogens from contaminating your substrate, you'll need to sterilize it thoroughly. For beginners, buying a mushroom grow kit, or having all the labor done for you, is an even more comfortable and convenient option. Supra kits from Zativo include no substrate and are entirely made up of pure mycelium. This is beneficial since it allows for more consistent harvesting. Add in the convenience of use, and this kit is ideal for a first harvest. The bag includes a ventilation system and needs to be sprayed with water every now and again. The boxes in the kit must be placed in the bag provided for this purpose, with the packet's opening on the table. The container must be folded and placed in sunshine, out of direct sunlight, at a temperature of around 28 degrees Celsius. Spray the sides of the inside of the bag with a spray to include the humidity required for its habitat. It only takes a few showers every day. After a week, you start to notice some indications of life. You should wait seven days for full growth after the first hats are visible. It's ready to harvest when this time has passed. When the "veil" is broken, this is the greatest time to do it. When the top of the mushroom cap opens and discharges its spores, the veil is broken. To avoid introducing a foreign life form into the growth media, which could endanger the health of your mushrooms, wash your hands before selecting them. Twist the mushrooms at the base of the culture bread where they develop very carefully and meticulously. The good news is that these kits allow you to harvest many times. Pour a little cold water on the culturing bread to shock the mycelium, and it will start growing again.

After 12 hours, remove the culture bread from the water and discard it. You're now ready to begin the various parts of the procedure outlined above.

Psilocybin Mushrooms Grown on Tree Trunks

Growing mushrooms on tree trunks is best done in shady areas of the garden. You'll discover how to grow tasty mushrooms in the wild right here. Anyone who has a garden and occasionally needs to remove a tree is likely to be stumped as to where to place the wood. The tree is used optimally and is easy to care for when mushrooms are grown on tree trunks. Here you will discover how to produce fresh mushrooms on your doorstep with little effort over a long period of time. Mushrooms can be grown on tree trunks. The most original and natural method of psilocybin mushroom culture is the cultivation of mushrooms on wood, which was originated thousands of years ago in Southeast Asia, particularly in Japan and China. Shiitake mushrooms (Lentinula edodes) were brought as a special gift to the country's monarchs and emperors. In traditional Chinese medicine, mushrooms are still used extensively, and medicinal mushrooms on tree trunks were first cultivated. We've put up a guide on how to cultivate mushrooms in your garden using wood.

The Best Psilocybin Mushroom Growing Wood

The majority of mushrooms prefer hardwoods including beech, oak, and birch, as well as all fruitwoods. They eat cellulose and lignin, the chemicals that give wood its strength and hardness. Even the thickest trunks disintegrate over time, and deadwood is recycled into organic stuff. Conifers, on the other hand, have thick, sticky resins that most edible mushrooms avoid. The exception is the smoky-leaved sulfur head (Hypholoma capnoides), which prefers spruce but less frequently pine and silver fir. The wood for the mushroom trunks should be cut as fresh as possible and preserved for at least two months, but no more than four. The wood's trunk diameter should be between 20 and 30 centimeters, and its length should be between 50 and 100 centimeters. Otherwise, the trunk will get very dry. Shiitake mushrooms require a stem with a diameter of 10 to 15 cm. The bark should be left as unbroken as possible since it helps to preserve moisture in the wood later. The trunk is now irrigated for two to three days, with the goal of completely covering it with water.

Which Mushrooms Are There?

Are They Appropriate for Cultivation? Mushrooms are a remarkably varied group of organisms. They eat food, ripe compost, and fallen huge trees. You naturally choose mushrooms that prefer to degrade wood while cultivating mushrooms in the garden. For your convenience, we've compiled a list of the most significant types.

Mushroom with oysters (Pleurotus ostreatus)

When young, it forms pressed-down hats that are folded up at the edges, making it one of the most well-known tree-living edible mushrooms. Pigeon blue, grey, white, and light brown are among the colors available. Its flavor is great and moderate, making it ideal for soups, sauces, and meat preparations.

Samtfubrübling / Enoki (Flammulina elutipes)

An edible mushroom with gleaming honey-colored tints that darken toward the core that is particularly popular in Japan. Without light, it produces elongated, colorless fruiting bodies that are cultivated in containers and sold solely in stores.

The flavor is delightfully sweet and mild. Mushroom rose (Pleurotus jammer)

It's also known as a flamingo mushroom because of its gentle pink tint. The fungus has a fan-shaped, lamellar fruit body with a velvety surface and a delicate mushroom flavor, and it is linked to oyster mushrooms.

Lemon yellow mushroom / Lemon mushroom (Pleurotus citrinopileatus)

Oyster mushrooms are closely related to this light yellow edible fungus, as seen by the shape of the fruiting bodies. It has a lemony flavor that makes it a great side dish for fish or salads.

The only edible fungus, the smoky-leaved sulfur head (Hypholoma capnoides), prefers to colonize conifers like spruce and pine. The nutty, spicy flavor of the yellow-brownish fruiting bodies. Because they share the same woodlands as the edible mushroom, there is a potential of misunderstanding with other, toxic sulfur head species.

Shiitake (Lentinula edodes) is a fawn-colored edible fungus with light flakes on a spherical cap and a light brown-whitish stem that is often used in Asian cuisine for its umami flavor. It must be grown as an aerial culture without the use of soil.

CHAPTER TWO
RECOMMENDED SOURCES OF SUPPLY
CULTIVATION TECHNIQUES

Finished mushroom mycelium is frequently sold as a "grain" or "cereal" product. The fungus spreads its mycelium throughout the rye, wheat, or other grain until it is completely covered. The grain brood is extremely easy to dose and immediately colonizes the wood. Inoculation dowels are untreated wooden dowels on which a certain mushroom variety was grown. The mushroom mesh has grown through the entire wood here as well. Both variations are appropriate for the development of tree trunks. Ready-made psilocybin mushroom brood is now available, primarily on the Internet - but lately also in hardware stores and garden centers - for growing on tree trunks.

We've put together a list of German supplier options for you. For numerous years, the mushroom parcel has been shipping several types of mushrooms from Nuremberg as a gift. Furthermore, mycelia can be purchased in the city. Since 2013, Mushrooms & Equipment Shop, based in Münsterland, has offered a wide range of kinds for hobby growers as well as commercial growth. Here you'll find vaccination dowels and cereal broods. Grain brood and inoculation dowels are produced in organic quality by a mushroom male from Saxony. The Dehner Garden Center now offers cultivation packages as well. Pilz Wald - The Pilzmanufaktur in Cologne offers a variety of mushrooms for the cultivation of tree trunks inoculated wooden dowels in its online shop.

Vaccinating the Trees

To inoculate the tree trunk, you'll need the following items, depending on the type of inoculation: • A chainsaw is required.

• A drill for wood

• A cordless screwdriver or a drill

A hammer is required.

• Tape or foil

• The mushroom brood in question The drill is used to drill holes in the prepared trunk with a diameter of around eight millimeters for the so-called dowel inoculation with mixed mushroom dowels. They should not, however, be more extensive than inoculation plugs. With a hammer, the dowels are carefully hammered into the hole. A wood drill with a drilling diameter of around 20 millimeters and a grain brood are required for the borehole method. This sort of mushroom brood has the benefit of spreading faster and more safely in the trunk than the mushroom dowel brood. Fill the mushroom brood with a pestle after drilling the holes and lightly compact it - the future mushroom stem is ready. The cut vaccination procedure necessitates one meter longer trunks. The log is sawed two or three times from below or above across its whole length. Then you use adhesive tape to cover the entire area. You can also staple the tape to make it more secure. Cut a small window in the adhesive tape to fill in the grain brood, then carefully fill in the grain brood and compact it a little. Finally, the inoculated trunk is wrapped in transparent film and pierced liberally with a nail or something similar. This stage is necessary to ensure that the stem keeps enough moisture for the fungus while still receiving oxygen. The trunks can also be stored under a plastic cover, although the humidity must be monitored more frequently in this case. Logs should be kept. As long as the fungus has not been able to develop through the trunk, newly inoculated wood is not yet hardy. It takes two to six months for the fungus to settle in its new home environment at 10 to 25 ° C, depending on the variety of mushroom. During this time, the trunk should be kept in the dark and often checked for dampness. If mold appears on the surface of the wood, the log is either too damp or the ventilation is inadequate. The unwelcome fungal attack will go away if you move the trunk to a more open location.

In the garden, arrange tree trunks.

You can see the fungus' mycelium emerging around the injection site if the wood has completely grown through. Now is the best time to remove the film or tape from the garden and set up the wood. All of the species mentioned, with the exception of the Shiitake, require touch with the dirt to form fruiting bodies. To do this, the trunks are buried a third to half way in the earth in a shady location. Earth culture is another name for this sort of gardening. Shiitake cultures, on the other hand, do not require a substrate to grow since their trunks are propped up against a fence or wall, a technique known as aerial culture. Shiitake mushrooms must be activated in order to produce fruiting bodies. The entire trunk is first immersed in cold water for 24 hours. Then you push it three to four times into the ground, which encourages fruiting. Patience is now essential, as the trunks normally do not require any extra attention, but do require a significant amount of time. On hot, dry days, the mushrooms, on the other hand, appreciate a little water around and on the stem. Now it's time to wait for the first fruiting bodies to appear. Because it currently takes anywhere from 6 to 24 months, depending on the variety of mushroom, to harvest for the first time.

Psilocybin Mushrooms Can Be Grown At Home

Mycelium, or the talus or nourishment mechanism of the fungus, which is made up of a collection of filaments or hyphae, is used to obtain the psilocybin mushroom. The psilocybin mushroom's fertile component is the so-called hymenium, which is made up of sheets in the lower part of the stem. The mycelium carries the spores (also known as conidia in fungi) that, once produced, produce new fungi. It is obtained in blocks in specialized scores for its extremely simple application. Another interesting fact is that mushroom pickers in the field use net bags to transport the specimens. While searching for mushrooms, they discharge the mycelium that will be utilized to produce future crops into the earth remains clinging to them. Psilocybin mushroom growing takes place in dark places (caves, basements, cellars, etc.) in specially designed bags or drawers. The drawers should be half a meter broad, a quarter meter high, and another quarter meter deep. As a substrate, we employ a combination that we keep in drawers in the following layers:

• The first layer consists of a third of a third of a third of a third of a third of a third of (preferably wheat, but also serves barley or oats).

• A third of a pear is mixed with sawdust for the second layer on top of the first. Sandalized soil is another alternative.

• Third layer: the entire area is technically coated with well-shredded manure. Use of cavalry manure is another alternative. We crumble the mycelium over the last layer of manure after the substrate has been laid in the drawers. Then we cover everything with a thin layer of peat and water, but not too much, to prevent mold growth. From now on, water frequently but not copiously, as previously stated, ideally with a spray gun or watering can rather than a water jar. Psilocybin mushroom cultivation necessitates the presence of darkness (light kills them). The drawers are subsequently placed in the cellar or basement of our choice (they can be piled on top of each other). ensuring that there is always a constant level of ambient humidity: The ideal humidity for this crop is 80%, which we can regulate with a hygrometer. It is also vital to have adequate ventilation. We must not allow the temperature to rise above 20 degrees Celsius. Anyone interested in improving their food supply should try growing mushrooms at home. Fungi are a healthy addition to any diet because they are low in calories and fat, high in fiber, and high in potassium and selenium. Fungi grow better indoors because light and temperature conditions are easier to manage. To grow mushrooms, the most important thing to understand is how to carefully control the requirements for their growth. Mushroom cultivation is straightforward, and once they begin to date, we can have continuous output until the nutrients in the preparation run out. Even so, some prior measures must be made to ensure that our crop is not infected with illnesses that render our harvest ineffective.

Irrigation

During the growing phase, the cloth covering should be sprayed with water several times every day. You keep wetting the earth, but never the mushrooms. It is critical to pay attention to water quality. Although rainwater is the safest option, mineral water is required. Then it'd be preferable if you sprayed the field at least twice a day.

Cultivation of Psilocybin Mushrooms on Coffee Grounds

You can grow mushrooms at home with a little patience and some coffee grounds. We show how the forest residents are procured, cared for, and harvested. Every day, coffee grounds end up in the garbage or, at the absolute least, in the compost. The nutrient-rich remains of a daily cup of coffee is also suitable for cultivating a broad range of mushrooms, which is yet relatively unknown. The next sections will teach you everything you need to know about growing psilocybin mushrooms on coffee grounds. On coffee grounds, a psilocybin mushroom grows. You can even breed the amusing forest inhabitants in the kitchen, as simple as that may sound. We'll teach you how to grow mushrooms on coffee grounds in the video below.

Coffee grounds for growing psilocybin mushrooms

Coffee grounds, which are high in nutrients, are increasingly being utilized as a substrate for edible mushrooms for ethical reasons. We eat just under 1% of the biomass of the original coffee bean when we drink a cup of coffee. The rest is still a great warm-scented substrate. Instead of garbage, it should be thrown in the bed and pots. Because coffee grounds are high in nitrogen, they can be used as a fertilizer for both mushrooms and plants. Small organisms in the soil degrade organic materials fast and easily, making it available to the plants. Here's a link to a specific article about using coffee grounds as a plant fertilizer. The hot brewing method also frees the coffee grounds of unwanted microbes like mold and bacteria, which is beneficial for psilocybin mushroom production. Filter coffee grounds are extremely well-suited to psilocybin mushroom production. As is generally the case with fresh beans, there aren't many antifungal compounds left. The remains from the self-grinding espresso machine are less conducive to mushroom growth. It's best if the coffee grounds aren't more than two to three days old. Otherwise, the likelihood of mold invasion rises once more. Freezing fresh sets eliminates this to a significant extent, allowing you to build up a small stock.

What goes into making a psilocybin mushroom?

Because it lives beneath the earth and rarely dares to come to the surface, the fungus is mostly invisible to humans. A true network of mushroom cells, known as hyphae, grows under and between the roots of trees in delightfully moist and nutrient-rich forest soils. Mycelium is the collective name for all cells that resemble a dense network of the most delicate roots. The mycelium of the mushroom communicates with neighbors and trees underground, digests organic debris, and releases nutrients from the soil. The psilocybin mushroom produces fruiting bodies as the weather becomes humid, cooler, and darker, such as in fall. They then appear in the form of mushrooms, delighting both animals and human collectors. The mushroom mycelium uses the umbrella-shaped or spherical fruiting bodies alone for reproduction. Thousands of spores are released above ground for the following generation, and the fungus itself is no longer visible within a few weeks. Mycelium meshes can grow to be genuine giants, weighing several tons and covering many square kilometers. The mycelium of the mushroom must be made to develop fruiting bodies in order to grow psilocybin mushrooms at home.

Psilocybin Mushroom Brood for Sale

You'll need some mycelium to start your psilocybin mushroom cultivation, which is normally on a little piece of wood or substrate. Because it is used to "inoculate" the substrate with the mushroom and allow it to grow through, this dried, convenient unit is also known as mushroom brood or vaccine brood. The mycelia starters are available in a variety of internet stores, sometimes as streaky wooden dowels or loose in plastic bags. Coffee grounds can, of course, be fed to mushroom growth sets with a finished substrate. On the internet, you can find a variety of mushroom-growing options. However, there are rising sets for the most diverse forms of mushrooms at several garden centers. We've hand-picked some German suppliers for you. Psilocybin mushroom packets have been transporting various species of mushrooms out of Nuremberg for several years now, as well as brood for breeding coffee grounds. Throughout addition, the mycelia can be purchased in the city. Since 2013, Mushrooms & Equipment Shop, based in Münsterland, has offered a wide range of kinds for hobby growers as well as commercial growth. Certified organic mushroom substrates, notably for growing on coffee grounds, are sent out by a mushroom guy from Saxony. The Dehner Garden Center now offers cultivation packages as well.

Grow Your Own Psilocybin Mushroom

If you want to try your hand at growing psilocybin mushrooms, you should be aware of the following points.

What kinds are appropriate? Mushrooms come in a variety of shapes and sizes, with some feeding on wood, leaves, or partially decomposed organic materials. Find out which sorts of bacteria can live on coffee grounds in your home. 'Oyster mushroom' is a term used to describe a type of fungus that grows (Pleurotus ostreatus) When young, these edible mushrooms grow in clusters from the substrate and create flat, depressed hats with rolled edges. Pigeon blue, grey, white, and light brown are the colors available. They're also known as veal mushrooms because of their consistency. Their flavor is great and moderate, making them ideal for soups, sauces, and meat preparations. 'Lemon yellow mushroom'/'Lemon mushroom' (Pleurotus citrinopileatus) Oyster mushrooms are closely related to this light yellow edible fungus, as seen by the shape of the fruiting bodies. The flavor is highly reminiscent of lemon, making it an excellent side dish for fish or salads. 'Roseseitling' (Pleurotus jammer) is also known as the flamingo mushroom because of its gentle pink tint. The mushroom, which is related to oyster mushrooms, has a fan-shaped, lamellar fruit body with a velvety surface and a delicate mushroom flavor — it may be used in a variety of ways. Shiitake (Lentinula edodes) is a fawn-colored edible fungus with light flakes on a spherical cap and a light brown-whitish stem that is often used in Asian cuisine for its umami flavor. It can be used in a variety of dishes. Agrocybe cylindracea ('Pioppino'/'Südlicher Ackerling') is a brown-capped, medium-sized edible fungus with a white stem that grows naturally on poplar trees. It has a nutty, chestnut-like flavor and firm meat, and it can be prepared in the same way as wild mushrooms.

Growing Psilocybin Mushrooms: Location and Climate

Edible mushroom growing thrives in cool environments with temperatures about 10 to 15 degrees Celsius and the highest potential humidity. Mushrooms thrive in the confines of a miniature greenhouse. Direct sunshine, as well as drying out the substrate, should be avoided. Mushrooms require some light to develop properly, although only fairly bright light is required. If the substrate is near a window, you must ensure that there are no drafts, as the fungi cannot tolerate this.

Mycelium Inoculation and Maintenance

First and foremost, the dry substrate must be soaked in water overnight to encourage mycelium growth. Wooden dowels that have been inoculated with bacteria are usually moist enough to be placed directly into the coffee grounds. The moist substrate is now combined with coffee grinds in a basin. The ratio of coffee grounds to inoculation substrate should be around 8:2. Fine wood particles or straw also help to loosen the mixture and maintain a proper water balance. Fill a flower pot, a bag, or a large glass halfway with the mixture and cover lightly to allow air to escape. Another option is to drill holes in the lid or use toothpicks to perforate the bag. The mycelium must now be allowed to grow completely through the substrate. It usually takes two to three weeks. Meanwhile, you should always check for adequate moisture and, if necessary, add some cold tap water. Waterlogging, on the other hand, must be prevented. The mycelium may die if this does not happen. Now is the time to wait since the first fruiting bodies will appear gradually after another 10 to 14 days. In order for the mushroom culture to grow out of the bags, the plastic must be cut with an X-shaped knife.

Psilocybin Mushroom Harvest

One can anticipate the harvest as soon as the first mushrooms appear. The downward curving edge of some species, like as the sidelines, gradually unrolls with increasing size before tearing. Now is the best moment to remove the mushrooms, either with a sharp knife or by twisting them gently by hand. Harvesting should begin as soon as the spores of the fruiting bodies have fallen out and are visible as a brownish-grey coating under the caps. Because the psilocybin mushroom has completed its mission and will die in a short period of time. After all of the fruiting bodies have been picked, the substrate should be allowed to adequately absorb water. The fruit reappears after a while. The nutrients in the coffee grinds are mostly used up after one or two harvest waves, depending on the amount, and must be replaced. The leached substrate can now be used as a mushroom brood by combining it with new coffee grounds and filling numerous jars with it. So you'll not only receive your edible mushrooms, but you'll be able to grow and pass them on swiftly as well.

Making Use of Fresh Mushrooms

Unfortunately, the freshest mushrooms available do not survive long and should be stored in the refrigerator and used within three days. Of course, you can preserve your harvest by freezing, drying, or pickling it. When the exotic plants are added directly to the saucepan, though, the flavor lasts the longest. Edible mushrooms, on the other hand, can be eaten raw, providing a distinct flavor sensation.

Some Information to Consider

What we call a mushroom or fungus is just the "fruit" of a fungus that is not visible to the naked eye in its natural state. While the mushroom is a certain size, the fungus that creates it can be much larger and colonize the subsoil without our knowledge. Fungi belong to a different kingdom than animals and plants, hence their cultivation conditions are different. There are many different types of mushrooms, and in this case, we're working with a saprophytic fungus, which means it feeds on decomposing matter, so we'll need to create a habitat that encourages this: ideal humidity and heat conditions for the mycelium (the mass of hyphae that makes up a fungus' vegetative body) to colonize the organic matter.

CHAPTER THREE
MUSHROOMS COLLECTION

How to Tell the Difference Between Poisonous and Edible Mushrooms

Edible mushroom collecting and identification is a multi-faceted pastime. The collector is out in nature, traversing woodlands. A keen eye for flora, a sense of where to look, and knowledge of mushroom growth are all required. In addition, edible mushrooms are prepared, giving the activity a gastronomic flavor. The mushroom guide below expands on these and other suggestions. This is meant to broaden the reader's understanding of many types, investigate the collecting and behavior of the fungus in the forest, and provide general information on the fungus. What Are the Different Types of Mushrooms?

The presence of chlorophyll in plants distinguishes them. Carbohydrates or carbon dioxide are produced as a result of this process. This dye isn't found in mushrooms. This means that the plants are unable to be classed as such. The fungus, on the other hand, is not an animal. In biology, mushrooms have a definition. They're eukaryotic organisms. These have a skeleton made up of cells in them. A fungus can be a single cell, as in baker's yeast, or a multicellular mold or edible mildew, as in edible mildew. Several thousand species have been identified. One hundred eighty diseases that can cause individual specimens in humans have already been recognized. Alcohol, vitamin C, and citric acid are all manufactured using mushrooms. They make up 90% of the water and live by utilizing their surroundings. Organic nutrients, which are isolated from decaying plant residues, are absorbed.

Mushroom Collecting Tips and Tricks

Finding and identifying edible mushrooms is a hobby that takes some preparation. These can be purchased both online and in person. However, this article has additional tips and tactics to assist you in finding them more quickly.

Only include mushrooms that are known to exist.

When do you know you've found a specimen? If it can be shown beyond a reasonable doubt. This indicates that the seeker is familiar with the crop and can recognize it. Pictures must be seen and descriptions must be read in order for this to be achievable. It's also important to know whether the mushroom looks like poisonous or inedible species, and how to tell the difference if there's any uncertainty. Experts can help you search and decide. The mushroom picker is not required to travel through the woods alone. In society, the hobby is enhanced by a discussion. Experts or experienced specialists can provide on-site advice, as well as assistance in locating and recognizing items. The "loot" is then distributed fairly. Migration of mushrooms Almost every federal state has a location where professionals accompany newcomers around the forest and explain how to explore and find things. Showcase your discovery If you travel alone, you might know someone in the neighborhood or nearby who can assist you identify the different species of mushrooms. Offices or the Poison Information Center can also help you find experts. The general guideline is that only pleasant and non-toxic mushrooms should be eaten. These must be completely determined ahead of time. The specimens should only be washed after the determination to be able to perform this even after the trek.

On the Trail and in the Woods The Appropriate Moment The inclination finder will rapidly locate it in the woods. Mushrooms flourish in damp soil with moderate temperatures. Enough specimens can be found after a few rainy days followed by a temperate temperature. The proportion of water in the mushroom is too high if it has rained for a long time. The find would shortly decompose. The Best Place to Look for Information The beginner enters the grove. Near trees, there should be a search. Until November, poplar or birch trees are frequently home to a variety of species. Knowing about trees is also important in this regard. Of course, if you're looking for a "birch mushroom," you shouldn't look in the spruce grove. Pick Mushrooms The fungus is trimmed off above ground once it has been identified. On site, he will be freed of garbage and grime. After that, you can put it in a basket. The Find's Transport The basket's interior must not be overly cramped. On the one hand, the mushroom need space to breathe and does not have to contend with pressure from above. Starting with bags or bags is not recommended. There, the copies acquire print regions and deteriorate more quickly. Anyone who has discovered a great spot to search should not take all of the specimens. If numerous mushrooms are left standing, the chances of "offspring" increase. Mushrooms that are unknown or even toxic should be avoided. They may become well-known as a result of the forest. Mushrooms that have rotted can be left unharmed. Specimens that have been eaten by animals are the same. Those who have arrived at home should distribute the mushrooms as soon as possible to allow air to circulate. Within a day, the mushroom enthusiast cleans and processes the treasure. This must be checked for worm marks as well. If you don't want to cook the mushrooms right away, you'll need to make them durable. Private persons are also prohibited from transporting mushrooms. A maximum quantity is set depending on the federal state, which ranges from one to two kilograms each day. Commercial trade is not included. You should only gather what you can eat yourself. The preservation and protection of existing species is also a concern for legislators. A penalty of up to 5,000 Euros can be imposed for transgression. It is also forbidden to search in gated woodland areas. The same is true for national parks, public parks, natural reserves, and wood-cutting districts.

Mushroom Identification

Differentiate between edible and poisonous specimens. Anyone who buys mushrooms in a supermarket believes they are edible. Anyone who collects mushrooms in the woods, on the other hand, does not always know if a fungus is deadly. Many types of mushrooms have a similar appearance. For example, the forest mushroom, which is popular as an edible fungus, resembles the deadly dangerous tuber agarics. Again, the idea is to only collect mushrooms that are easily identifiable. The following performance is meant to help with this.

Identify Edible Plants and Animals

Every mushroom collector's goal is to find delectable mushrooms. Here's a first description to help you figure out what species you're dealing with. Because many mushrooms resemble one other, judging them just on the basis of text or even images from mobile phone apps is insufficient. Only going to the grove with an expert or showing the find to a professional is recommended.

Boletus is a character in the Greek mythology (Boletus edulis)

This species, sometimes known as a men's mushroom, has a reddish brown hat, a shiny look, and is slightly sticky. The brown-red stem is rough, bulbous, and taper somewhat towards the bottom. The meat is whitish in color. It has a somewhat irrational flavor and is loaded with vitamins and minerals. In the shadow of a tree, these specimens thrive. There's a chance you'll mix it up with the bitter porcini mushroom.

Chanterelle Chanterelle Chanterelle Chanterelle Chan (Cantharellus cibarius)

One of the most well-known edible mushrooms is the chanterelle. It has a distinct appearance. There is no difference between the hat and the stem as they sprout in one piece. It's a yellowish color. The stem and hat of this mushroom have grooves, which are typical of this species. The chanterelle grows in a funnel form most of the time. It grows near spruce, oak, beech, pine, and birch at high altitudes. chanterelle chanterelle chanterelle chanterelle chanterelle

Cantharellus infundibuliforme (Cantharellus infundibuliforme)

Because the fruiting body is hollow, the fungus is also known as perforated baby. Autumn chanterelle, on the other hand, is more common. Fir and spruce forests are his natural habitat, as long as the soil is sufficiently acidic. Colors include yellow, grey, and ocher brown.

Champignon de forêt (Agaricus sylvatic)

It appears to be the same as the supermarket version. The hat's maximum circumference is ten centimeters. The hat of the mushroom is characterized by ocher colors, brown threads, and scales. Even in little specimens, the head remains spherical. The stem can be as thick as eight centimeters. Despite its name, the Waldchampignon mushroom is frequently found in gardens and parks, where picking is forbidden.

Morels for food (Morchella esculenta)

These specimens have a head that closely resembles a honeycomb and are quite tasty but difficult to hunt down in the woods. Because it prefers acidic soil, it can only be found in floodplain woods. Spring is when morels bloom. There's a chance you'll get mixed up with the toxic spring Lorchel.

Sponges made of cane (Kuehneromyces mutabilis)

It's a mushroom that goes well in soups. It feeds on decaying wood. On the edge of the hat, there are small grooves. The skin is white and the tint ranges from light to dark brown. This is the only type that should be collected by connoisseurs. When it comes to poison ducks, there's a good chance you'll get them mixed up. These appear on the hardwood as well.

Mushroom with butter (Suillus luteus)

It belongs to the edible mushroom genus. This form of fungus, however, is not suitable for everyone. It is sometimes referred to as "dangerous to one's health." It can be found in the vicinity of pine trees. The hat's adhesive layer, which must be removed before collection, is distinctive. The coloration can begin yellowish and progress to a chocolate brown.

Hallelujah! (Armillaria mellea)

This genus has a diverse range of mushrooms. The stem is largely made up of cotton. This condition may pass depending on the weather. The fungus is capable of killing trees. It ranges in color from yellowish to brownish in appearance. The mushroom kind prefers to grow in tree cavities. The stem is 20cm long and has a higher height.

Autumnal horns (Craterellus cornucopioides)

This fungus, which is also known as a trumpet, is still edible. It's frequently used as a seasoning. This is why some people make a powder out of it. It's related to chanterelles, has a trumpet shape, and can grow up to twelve centimeters in diameter. Brown, grey, and black are all shades of the same color.

The ear of Judas (Auricularia auricula-judge)

Chinese morel is a mushroom that can be found in Asian restaurants. The mushroom does not have a strong flavor. It is, nonetheless, prized for its high nutritional content. It is utilized for medical purposes throughout Asia. It has the ability to regulate blood circulation, among other things. The mushroom is shaped like an auricle and has a somewhat felted upper body. It can be found all year on both living and dead trees (also in Germany). It can be found on elderberry trees in abundance.

Boletus Chestnut (Xerocomus badius)

This color designation, sometimes known as the brown cap, provides a color description. However, the body is similarly brown in hue. Underneath the hat is a yellow sponge that becomes azure when pushed. Because this mushroom is dangerous when raw, it should be thoroughly cooked.

Mushroom of the birch (Leccinum scabrum)

With a hat width of up to 15 cm, this mushroom is named after the location where it was discovered. The color is grey-brown, but it can also be yellowish or reddish in tone. The hat bulges with maturity, whereas the young mushroom seems spherical. The stem can grow up to 15 cm long.

Cap made of red oak (Leccinum quercinum)

An orange hat with a diameter of up to 25 cm. It also has a bright yellow hue to it. The stem is white to grey in hue, with brown or orange markings. It's a rare fungus that can only be found in the shade of oak trees. When the fungus is cooked, it turns black.

Bolete with red feet (Xerocomus chrysenteron)

The consistency of edible mushrooms might alter over time. As a young mushroom, the red-footed bolete is delicious. It features a dark olive-green convex cap. When the fungus reaches an elderly age, it turns grey-brown. The stems are thin and golden. There is a little red glint can be found. In both coniferous and deciduous forests, mushroom species cluster together.

Boletus in Gold (Suillus grevillea)

If the weather is nice, this mushroom genus might appear in big groups. They're mostly found under the shade of larch trees. The stem is usually thin and orange, yellow, or reddish-brown in color. The hat takes on the same hue as the shirt. The hat's underside is stained. Before placing the specimen in the basket, the slimy skin should be peeled off.

Lycoperdon perlatum (Bottle Dustling)

The mushroom is shaped like a bottle and has a spherical head. The plants are incredibly white when they are young. Later on, they take on a yellow or olive hue. It is possible to eradicate warts on the fruiting body. Folds can be seen on the stem. Bottle dust is a common phenomenon in both coniferous and deciduous forests. It's best to consume it when it's still young.

Bolete of hornbeam (Leccinum pseudoscabrum)

This variety of mushroom has a hemispherical hat that can reach a length of up to 15 centimeters and is usually light brown in color.

• Depending on age and weather, a smooth surface can crack.

• It blooms from July to October, mostly among hornbeams.

• Collectors should inspect the fungus for maggots as a precaution. Mushrooms that are delicious can also be preserved. The boletus, all types of chanterelle, the birch mushroom, the hornbeam boletus, and the food morel are among the specimens mentioned here. It is also possible to gather these mushrooms. However, only a maximum of one kilogram is allowed. Knowing how to identify a find is crucial for collecting and, more importantly, for consuming. Even edible mushrooms can be toxic if not cooked thoroughly.

Mushrooms That Aren't Poisonous or Digestible

Mushrooms are not just categorized into "edible" and "toxic" categories. There are a few examples that can be eaten, however they do not have the flavor of an edible fungus. They are, however, an important part of the ecology. Below is a list of some of the most well-known specimens.

False chanterelle chanterelle chanterelle chanterelle chant (Hygrophoropsis aurantiaca)

This mushroom's hat diameter is 19 cm, and its head bulges gently until it resembles a funnel. In elderly age, the specimen receives waves. It comes in a variety of colors ranging from yellow to orange. Slats run the length of the stem. The stem can grow up to six centimeters in length and is somewhat hollow. This type of mushroom can be found in coniferous and deciduous woodlands from August through November. This "bluff pack" isn't meant to be consumed. The fungus might have a harmful impact on digestion.

Gall's face flushes (Tylopilus files)

The head can reach a length of up to 20 centimeters. The mushroom is yellow to reddish-brown in hue. The tubes are available in a variety of colors ranging from greyish white to light pink. The meat is whitish in color. It grows under conifers and is frequently confused with porcini. It is possible for a dish to be spoilt if only a small amount of bilberry bolete is used.

Tinting for Woodpeckers (Coprinus picaceus)

A dark brown hat with white dots on the brim. It turns black as it gets older. The stem is relatively long and thin. It can only be found in deciduous woodlands. It's virtually always possible to find it on its own.

Bunting in verdigris (Stropharia aeruginosa)

The mushroom wears a six-centimeter-wide hat. A bluish-green color with varying tints is usual. This includes the hat's surface as well as the stem. On the specimen is a thin, detachable mucosal membrane. In both deciduous and coniferous forests, this fungus can be found.

Ringed Flämmling is a type of flämmling with a (Gymnopilus junonius)

When the child is small, the head resembles half of a spherical. Later, an elongated hat with a width of up to 15 centimeters is developed. The color ranges from golden yellow to apricot. The stem is slender at first, then grows bulbous in the middle. The stem is the same color as the hat. Ringed flamingos can be spotted on tree trunks, usually under older deciduous trees.

Youngling squabbling (Pholiota squarrosa)

The cap is slightly raised. The hat and stem base are pale yellow to orange in color. The top of the stem is completely naked. The hat is coated in scales that are clearly apparent. On and around tree stumps, the specimen can be found. It also builds its nest in gardens.

Mushrooms That Are Poisonous Not all toxin-producing fungi are dangerous. Nausea, headaches, dizziness, and other symptoms are possible side effects. If you eat the incorrect kind of mushroom, you could die. However, there is frequently a window of opportunity to intervene. This is covered in more detail below in a different section. The following list of inedible mushrooms has been segmented once more to provide a general overview. The first section is about dangerous animals. Other dangerous mushrooms are also listed, with symptoms best described. This section demonstrates better than anyone else why learning to identify fungi is so important for a collector. Experts also seek safety guidance.

Mushrooms That Kill

The green tuber agaric (Amanita phalloides) hat can be three to fifteen centimeters wide. It comes in a variety of shapes, from egg-shaped to bell-shaped. The coloration comes in a variety of tones of olive. The stem can grow to be as long as 16 cm. There is a zigzag pattern visible. Although the meat has a lovely nutty aroma, even small amounts can cause severe illness. You will die of liver coma if you overeat. The lag ranges from eight to forty hours. Symptoms include nausea, vomiting, and diarrhea. The white tuber agaric (Amanita virosa) produces an egg that develops into a hat with a diameter of up to ten centimeters. The scent is sweet, and the color is white. From June through September, the fungus can be found in coniferous forests. Things's easy to mix it up with the mushroom. A few grams of tapered tuberous agaric, also known as tapered tuberous agaric, can cause lethal amatoxin syndrome. The damage to the kidneys and liver is permanent. The mushroom genus Amanita verna develops a hemisphere at first, but eventually the hat becomes convex. Specimens are occasionally recessed in the centre. In an ocher, a smooth body is usual. It is possible to obtain a width of ten centimeters and a height of fifteen centimeters. His specialty is deciduous and mixed woodland, which can also be found in parks. From May through September, the deadly poisonous mushroom can be found. From 30 grams onwards, liver failure is to be predicted.

Toadstools are a type of mushroom (Amanita muscaria) A well-known fungus with a lovely look that is, nevertheless, lethal. The hat is red with light flakes and measures up to 30 cm in diameter. The hue of the hat can range from orange to yellow. The meat has a wonderful odor here as well. This fungus can be found on spruce and birch trees from July through October. The cardiovascular system will collapse in the worst-case scenario, and the breathing system will become paralyzed. Paxillus involutus (Bald Krempling) This specimen is also known as bacon mushroom. This term comes from the glossy surface. The hat has a width of up to 15 centimeters. It is possible to reach a height of nearly 20 cm. The stem is white, yellow, or brownish-red, and the underside is white, yellow, or brownish-red. The hat is brown with a yellow or red tint to it. These specimens can be found in coniferous and deciduous groves from June to November. If consumed on a frequent basis, bald Kremling can cause an antigen-antibody reaction in the body. In the long run, this can lead to death. Panther mushrooms (Amanita pantherina) have a light to dark brown or grey color with a width of up to twelve centimeters. White flakes on it can be readily removed with a damp cloth. It can take the shape of a half ball, a domed mushroom, or a flat mushroom. The maximum height is 12 cm. From July through October, the specimen can be seen in coniferous and deciduous woodlands. Nausea, vomiting, and diarrhea can occur if you consume more than 100 grams. There is a state of intoxication, which can lead to coma or death due to respiratory paralysis. The brick-red crack mushroom (Inocybe erubescens) can be found in parks, gardens, and along paths. However, the fungus can be found in deciduous forests with a width of nine centimeters and a height of eight centimeters. It is white, yellow, or ocher in color. It's possible to make a blunt cone up to the size of a conventional bell. It grows in limestone soil alongside ivy and blooms from May to August. 40 to 500 grams, depending on the muscarin level of the mushroom, are lethal. A little mushroom with a maximum width of four centimeters and a stem length of at least seven centimeters is known as a harmful pest (Galerina marginata). The color ranges from pale brown to ocher. The head might flatten down or form a bell shape. From July through November, these plants grow mostly on tree stumps in coniferous, deciduous, and mixed forests. The result is a reduction in blood pressure, passing, an increase in pulse, and liver injury. A deadly dose is said to be between 100 and 150 grams. The orange-foxed woodchuck (with a two-week latency period), the hunched-up woodchuck, ergot, the spring salmon, the hazel-brown umbrella, and the gorgeous yellow clubfoot are all lethal mushrooms. With thousands of mushroom varieties, this performance is likewise inconclusive.

Mushrooms That Are Poisonous The term Kartoffelbovist (Scleroderma citrinum) comes from the shape of the potato head. Skin that is coarse and warty, in tones of green, grey, or ocher, is typical. From old age to black, there is a wide spectrum of colors to choose from. His abode is unlimed, acidic soil. Gastrointestinal symptoms are rather common. Consumption can potentially result in fainting. Mica ink (Coprinus micaceus) has a white to greyish tint on the specimen with the thin stem and bell-shaped head. It's a mushroom with a hollow interior. Anti-bus poisoning can occur as a result of consuming alcohol. From spring until autumn, this type of fungus can be found growing everywhere. Boletus, Satan (Boletus Satanas) Ordinary is a full and broad hat in the shape of a hemisphere with a width of up to 25 cm. The pores are reddish in tone, and the head appears greyish white to leather-colored. The flesh is white to yellow and the stem is thick. Following the increase, gastrointestinal symptoms are expected. When mushroom hunting, the champion Carbole Egerling (Agaricus xanthoderma) is a common target. This genus includes the Karbonegerling, which is venomous. The fungus has a dazzling white appearance. Slats can be found beneath the head. This toadstool is frequently found growing in the undergrowth. The boarding turns chrome yellow when the tuber is sliced. Diarrhoea is a side effect of the rise. Seizures and disorientation are other possible side effects. Green-leaved sulfur head (Hypholoma fasciculare) is a fungus with a maximum height of ten centimeters and a width of up to seven centimeters. His hat is a yellowish-green color that darkens in the middle. The stem has a yellow hue to it. From May to December, the mushroom species can be found on decaying wooden ground. In this case, the stomach and intestines are also damaged. Other toadstools include the zigzag-red crack fungus, spotted pigeon, enormous redlining, purple thick-footed, and alkaline redlining (this list is by no means complete).

How Does the Psilocybin Mushroom Work?

How Do Pickers Act in the Woods? Seekers should maintain a peaceful demeanor so as not to upset the animal kingdom. Sturdy footwear and weather-appropriate attire are required. Kneeling is a good idea if you want to recognize the mushrooms. The only instruments required are a mushroom knife for collection, a basket to transport the find, and a book for identification. Garbage is not disposed of in the forest, as should be obvious. Picking mushrooms is illegal in nature reserves. The wonderful trails must also not be abandoned. Unidentified mushrooms have remained. Anyone who captures pictures at home can try to identify them. When specimens are discovered, they are usually kept standing. Mushrooms will then continue to grow in that location in the future. Beginners should avoid agarics at all costs. This comprises a large number of toadstools. Mushrooms with a sponge, on the other hand, are perfectly safe. There aren't many toxic plants here. Anyone planning on going on additional hikes should make sure the car is found. Security can be provided via a compass and a cell phone. Also, relatives or acquaintances should be aware of your whereabouts.

When does the season for psilocybin mushrooms start and end?

Unfortunately, there is no way to know for sure. The mushrooms grow according to the weather, not our calendar. From May onwards, you can travel to the forest to pick mushrooms. This marks the start of the boletus period. In June, the chanterelle appears. The initial specimens often thrive in huge numbers in moist and warm weather. In August, the Bovist can be found. Mushrooms are edible mushrooms (not to be confused with the highly poisonous tuber agarics.) Have you started growing yet? The true psilocybin mushroom season, on the other hand, does not commence until the third season. Mushroom pickers are most active in September and October. At this season, the autumn trumpet, crayfish, chanterelles, chestnuts, Hallimasch porcini mushrooms, and the stick sponge have been spotted on the radar for edible mushrooms. These varieties, on the other hand, should only be eaten steamed or cooked. In theory, edible mushrooms can be found throughout the year. However, if these are harvested before their prime, they lose quality, nutritional value, and flavor. Wet and warm weather, as well as appropriate conditions, can advance the psilocybin mushroom season on the calendar.

This Is Correct If You've Consumed Poisonous Mushrooms

Those who get mushroom poisoning from eating their find must take the necessary precautions. 80% of the mushrooms discovered had been cooked wrongly. Other specimens can only obtain their potential to promote well-being when cooked, as edible mushrooms are typically difficult to tolerate raw. Up to 20% of complaints can be attributable to correct fungal poisoning. Gastric and intestinal illnesses are common, albeit the symptoms vary. The result is abdominal cramps, nausea, and diarrhea. Of course, this could also be the result of poor preparation. When mushrooms are reheated, they can become unbearable. Fungal poisoning is characterized by dizziness, heavy breathing, hallucinations, muscle twitching, restlessness, bewilderment, dread, rapid heartbeat, and cramping. If symptoms emerge within a few minutes or four hours, you should take action right away. A doctor should be contacted, or a poison control center should be established. Poisoning from tuberous agaric usually takes half a day to manifest.

Mushrooms that are edible can be stored and eaten later.

Mushrooms have a short shelf life. Processing should be done as soon as possible. Pressure, heat, and light are all sensitivities for the fungus. The chosen storage location should be comfortable. A night on the balcony, the refrigerator's vegetable compartment, or the cold cellar are suitable. Wild mushrooms, on the other hand, can only be described as fresh for a few days. The container must be able to breathe. When specimens degrade, they typically produce poisons. After washing the wild mushroom, it can be frozen. It's time to drain the samples. After that, they remain constant for about four months. The frozen items are reprocessed without being defrosted first. Dried mushrooms can also be used. This can be done in the oven at 40 degrees Celsius or, better yet, in a dehydrator. Prior to use, the discovery must be cleaned. Attention! If you don't care about storage, you should eat the wild mushroom within two or three days.

CHAPTER FOUR
MUSHROOM GROWING TIPS AND TRICKS

You Can Grow Your Own Edible Mushrooms There are various advantages to growing mushrooms yourself. When they're needed, they're harvested. It is not required to take a long trek through the woods. And the figure can be manipulated. Vegetarians, for example, benefit from shitake since it includes vitamin D, which is found primarily in meat. Mushrooms can be grown in a variety of methods, as seen below. Forest Garden: The mushrooms have their own space in the garden. It is a melting pot of cultures. Brown cap, herb mushroom, and oyster mushroom, for example, are all suited. They prefer to be in the shade. Hardwood: The wood is sawn here. In the opening, the mushroom brood is put. After that, the incision must be sealed. In this environment, oyster mushrooms, shitake mushrooms, and lime mushrooms thrive. Water and brood can be added to a straw bale. A shady location is ideal for oyster mushrooms, brown cap mushrooms, lime mushrooms, and herb mushrooms in this circumstance. Greenhouse: A greenhouse can be used to cultivate some crops. House: A wet location within the house, such as the basement, is ideal. Shadow is also necessary. Mushrooms and pioppinos, for example, are suitable. When purchasing crops, longevity is always a priority. This is usually something that needs to be done fast. More information about the cultivation must be received ahead of time.

• When is the best time to harvest?

• How much money can you anticipate to make?

• What are the ideal temperatures?

• What is the best place to grow the mushroom? The boletus, chanterelles, and morel, in addition to the famed champion, are successfully bred. To pluck mushrooms competently, the components mushroom brood, substrate, and cultivation circumstances must be united. Mycelium, the white substrate of mushrooms, is the mushroom brood. In comparable settings, this develops. The substrate refers to the material on which the growth will take place. Tree trunks, straw, and dirt are all options. The growth of the mycelium is the first step in the cultivation of a mushroom strain. The greater the substrate, the longer it takes to spread throughout the space. Mushrooms will eventually form if the humidity and temperature are just right. The fruiting body is generated by the sexual dispersion of spores, whereas the mycelium spreads asexually. The transportation is handled by water, wind, and animals. When cultivating mushrooms, it is not required to determine whether or not they are edible. Rather, hobby breeders must strive for proper preparation so that delight is not accompanied by discomfort. The mushrooms will grow swiftly under the correct conditions; enjoy your feast.

What Equipment Is Required?

• A pyrex pan box, which holds all of the ingredients and regulates the temperature.

• a stray (can be boiled to prevent the grain remnants from germinating).

• Compost your waste (so that the bacteria contained in it begin the work of decomposition).

• Water, which will be used to moisten the mixture.

• Cover it with peat or mulch.

• Grain mycelium is a type of mycelium that grows on grains (in our case of the Agaricus Bisporus variety, the mushroom from Paris).

• sawdust, straw, or manure (fungal mycelia)

• spray bottle

• baking tray

• heating pad

• leaf land

• Hand towel We favor mulch above peat because, despite its high nutrient content, we consider peat to be a non-renewable resource, comparable to oil or other types of coal, because its production needs thousands of years of decomposing plants. Their regeneration rate is comparable to that of the various chemicals. Before we begin, we must ensure that our hands and work utensils are clean, as contamination during the "sowing" procedure may impede the colonization of the fungus of interest against other fungi or bacteria that may be present. As a result, not only should you wash your hands, but you should also avoid coughing or sneezing near the mixture.

Process

1. In a bucket, combine the straw and compost, moistening it slightly as you stir. Coffee grounds can be added to this mixture because studies have shown that when used as a nutritional supplement, they can increase mushroom output by threefold.

2. We pour the mixture into the box and fill it almost to the brim. We supply more nourishment to our mushrooms the more we disguise it.

3. We sprinkle mushroom mycelium on the inoculated grains. 4. We cover the result with about a finger of wet mulch and sprinkle it with spray water to make sure it's well saturated. Once this process is complete, we must cover our box to prevent light from entering for a period of 5 to 8 days, or until the mycelium (represented by a whitish hair) has colonized the mixture's surface. We need to maintain our box moist during these days. We recommend not going overboard and pouring the water slowly with the help of a spray or diffuser. Meanwhile, we build a window in the lid (the height is sufficient for our mushrooms to develop) through which light can enter. To prevent the loss of moisture or heat, this window should be covered with a translucent plastic film that enables light to pass through.

Remember that it is not appropriate to place it where it will receive direct sunlight, but rather where it will receive indirect sunlight (on a closet, in an indoor patio). Once the process is complete, we keep our box at a temperature between 10 and 22 degrees, in a place without direct light, and with a humidity level of 80 percent, replicating the conditions of the undergrowth, natural habitat of Mushrooms and other fungi. We keep spraying water when we think it's important to keep the humidity up and the mushrooms growing for the next few days. We do it on the inside of the lid, not on the mushrooms, to keep the fungi from becoming wet and decomposing. It keeps the produce from getting too wet and may rot before harvest. When all the droplets in the lid have evaporated, we know you need water. The first mini-mushrooms begin to sprout after around 12 days. The first mature production occurs after 20 days, when the mushroom hat has grown to a diameter of 5-8 cm. Mushrooms should be harvested while the sheets under the hat are pink, as this indicates that they are starting to pass. We can collect the larger ones as we need them, keeping in mind that if we follow the procedure correctly, we should be able to harvest once a week. It is critical that we do not cut them in order to collect them; instead, we must twist the mushroom's body slightly to separate it from the substrate. The harvest lasts from October to March/April, depending on the temperature that we can maintain on the plantation. If it still keeps food after this date, it can last as long as the prescribed temperature is maintained. The cultivation of edible mushrooms in Latin America began around the end of the 1930s, and progress has been extremely slow during the next 50 years for a variety of reasons:

• The lack of information, distribution, and complete ignorance regarding the production of edible fungi by agricultural institutions at the time. As a result, there is a lack of fungus production and consumption. These conditions have created and continue to make this product an aristocratic cuisine, resulting in the mushroom industry's growth being almost unilateral. That is, those who began mushroom manufacturing at the time, built their businesses, and are now well-established in the market. This hermeticism and technological agoraphobia problem can be found in various Latin American countries that fail to grasp that success is found in the beginning, not the end. In the 1990s, several agribusiness producers of edible mushrooms developed in several Latin American countries, making the product less scarce and allowing for healthy competition in terms of quality and quantity, as well as the cost of the product to the final customer. In the mid-to-late 1990s, the organization of Fungi Expos and Conference Cycles on the Commercial Production of Edible Fungi started, bringing the general public into contact with firms that provide inputs and services. This eliminates the mystery around mushroom cultivation, allowing consumers interested in these crops to access accurate technical information and compare or purchase technology adapted to their specific needs. A BUM has emerged in the production of Pleurotus spp. mushrooms, as well as the proliferation of hundreds of small mushroom producers who have been taught and supported in good faith by universities and institutional programs to produce with a very agricultural system, in which those who take it on do so out of necessity. Others are victims of those who sell and promote this activity to do business by selling seed of dubious quality and produced in many cases in a rustic manner, and others are victims of those who sell and promote this activity to do business by selling their seed of dubious quality and produced in many cases in a rustic manner. As a result of all of this, only one product of variable quality and quantity exists. It is feasible to make the small clarification that the advisers do not have the essential experience in mushroom agribusiness. The difficulty is that there is no location to train, not because they don't want it or because of a lack of capacity. Currently, conditions have changed as a result of globalization, and Latin America is an up-and-coming large market for mushroom production, with many other European and North American countries desiring its requirements due to its low labor costs and plentiful raw materials for the production of this crop. The need for new food sources and the repurposing of abandoned structures As a result of APIADE (Use of Disused Agricultural Facilities), mushroom growing has become an alternative crop that boosts income for diverse producers or those who are solely focused on this crop.

Production Methodologies There are two types of psilocybin mushroom farming systems:

• Production System (Traditional or Rustic)

• System of Industrial Production

Production in the Old Ways

System The traditional production method is the most well-known and is widely practiced in most both urban and rural communities, thanks in part to university-based distribution. This manufacturing technique has proven to be the most popular due to its big attraction and advantage of minimal production investment. However, despite the low prices, various factors have forced manufacturers to abandon psilocybin mushroom production, resulting in the following negative effects:

• Establishment of integrated production units (IPUs): This means that anyone interested in growing this crop must study and monitor all of the processes in the most expensive manner possible (Trial and Error) Inadequate and expert counsel is lacking.

• Difficulty getting quality seed

• Shortcomings or deficiencies in facility adaption and management

• Low quantity and quality of output

• Unfair marketing competition

• Lack of organization in product distribution and sale

• Slow or nearly non-existent growth in production Because of these considerations, psilocybin mushroom cultivation in Mexico is no longer regarded a serious business, despite the fact that government and commercial institutions continue to promote it, as well as the national market's need as an international market.

PROCESSES OF CULTURE IN THE TRADITIONAL SYSTEM

A QUICK OVERVIEW OF AGRICULTURAL OUTPUT

The following procedures:

• Pasteurization (pasteurization)

• Planting

• Vaccination

• initiation

• Production Techniques In more detail:

1. Shake up the straw bales

2. Filling metal mesh molds with straw in bulk

3. Place metal molds with straw in a container with water at 80 degrees Celsius for two hours (pasteurization)

4. Drain and chill the molds by removing them with straw from the boxes filled with water.

5. Seed (inoculum) distribution on and between the straws (SEED)

6. Planting straw in plastic sacks weighing 10-12 kg. Average

7. Transport of plastic bags to hatcheries or culture halls (INCUBATION)

8. Temperature regulation and management for roughly 15 days at 24° C on average

9. Getting to the production halls

When you're in elementary school and have little or no cultural experience,

Advantages:

• Does not necessitate a significant financial investment

• It takes up very little room.

• In low-income communities, it is a diverse production choice.

• It's a self-consumption alternative for production.

• Agricultural shells are used Disadvantages:

• For the most part, each producer performs all production processes, which is too much technical information for someone with a low school education and little or no experience in agriculture, as well as the task of monitoring all of the processes involved in the crop, which is the most important and risky process.

• As a result, you can't seed more than 50 bags per day per container in this method, and increasing the output section of bags necessitates a larger number of boxes and, thus, a larger number of people, which leads to higher expenses and irregularities in the processes.

• Because of the low bag production, bags with planting dates ranging from 8 to 15 days apart must be concentrated to incubate in the same growing room, with the same treatments applied, when each item is required, or a quantity of seeded bags is kept with a single treatment, and because the different items of seeded bags are kept together, the applied therapy helps some and delays others.

• They frequently lack ventilation and temperature control systems, relying on natural ventilation at the expense of the environment.

• As a result, there is an irregular mushroom production with inconsistencies in size, quantity, and commercial grade, making it hard to enter a continuous marketing cycle. Commercial and Industrial Manufacturing

Advantages:

• The high cost of the investment necessitates extra caution and expert monitoring in both the cultivation and equipment installation processes, as well as the plant design and, if necessary, infrastructure adaption.

• The manufacture of bags It is significantly greater in a single game, for example: in a 15 x 3 x 3.5 mt tunnel filling at 1.5 meters high, around 1,200 bags of 15 kg each are generated, allowing the tunnel to be used up to twice a week without the substrate fermenting for so long.

• Special equipment maintains temperature and ventilation regulation, ensuring uniform quality across the 1,200 bags.

• It contains enough bags in the incubation and production vessels to deliver the same treatment to all of them at the same time.

• The production is uniform, ensuring a larger quantity and consistent quality of goods, allowing entry into the formal national or international market. Disadvantages:

• Commercial and industrial production technicians are in short supply.

• Will necessitate greater resources and space.

• It necessitates the use of machinery and equipment.

Pasteurization Tunnel Design and Construction

The tunnel is usually filled to a height of 1.6 to 1.8 meters, and if this height is exceeded, the compost may become anaerobic due to compacting. Because the compost cannot generate enough heat on its own, steam must be injected through a boiler. The tunnel filling work is not limited if it is filled with an endless belt, tractor, or manually because the height from the floor to the ceiling can be 3.5 to 4.0 meters. The whole total distance between the real floor and the false floor is less than 90 centimeters, which is inconvenient since this space is where the air and steam injection ducts are connected, and with a 2% slope along the tunnel, this space is where the air and steam injection ducts are connected. When building a psilocybin mushroom plant, it is necessary to plan ahead of time for the locations or spaces that will be occupied in the future so that the harmony and workflow diagram are not disrupted. The tunnel must have two entrances for sanitary reasons and a smooth operational flow. One door is at one end and is where the compost is carried to the sowing area, which is regarded a clean area, and the other entrance is at the other end and is where the compost is taken to the sowing area, which is often located outside near the composting yard. This flow chart reduces time spent filling tunnels and sowing seeds, as well as the risk of disease transmission from pasteurized compost coming into touch with filthy or decomposing areas. The difference between the pasteurization tunnel for psilocybin mushroom compost and the pasteurization tunnel for psilocybin mushroom compost is that the density of the compost is lower in the case of mushrooms, so it is essential to calculate the cubic meters, which is as follows:

• Psilocybin mushroom compost characteristics: 250-300 kg / mt3 density

• Fan performance: 200 mt3 / hr / ton.,

• A centrifugal fan, and a water column or pressure of 100-110 mm.

The Tunnel's Construction

A pasteurization tunnel can be made out of a variety of materials, such "W" panels (Dutch type) coated with plastic, greenhouse or Irish, or even the most typical, block or partition wall. To construct the first two types of tunnels, some firms sell the materials and others install them anywhere in the world. They are practical, durable, pleasant, aesthetic, and functional, but they must be ordered a few months ahead of time and take into account the transfer time. For those that plan their actions according to reality, the time it takes to place an order and get the material, equipment, or service is not inconvenient. The only potential drawback is that they may abandon the investment budget. A hole of this size of 3.0 mt can be excavated to begin the building of a tunnel (local type). The length was calculated with a minimum of 90 centimeters in the lowest portion and a slope of 2% till the end of the pit, while some left a minimum of 1.5 meters in the bottom part to fit a person to clean the tunnel's floor. Two lateral holes can be proportionally put along the tunnel in the plenary session to insert the ducts where the air will be injected. After the excavation is completed, the concrete or stone foundation is laid, and the concrete beams, which can be 4 "x 8" x 3.0 mt, are reloaded and placed next to each other with a 1 "space corresponding to 25% of the total floor area, are reloaded and placed next to each other with a 1 "space corresponding to 25% of the total floor area. Following that, two walls were built on each side, with a 5 centimeter gap between them, in which insulating materials such as Unicel, glass wool, polyurethane, and others were installed. Another solution can be made in areas where the earth is fairly hard and excavation is expensive or impossible, and it consists of lifting the walls and contemplating 90 centimeters above the floor. constructing a parapet in If the beams or wooden poles must be reloaded, it is preferable for the poles to be 4 "x 4" by 3 meters so that they can be withdrawn and reinstalled throughout the tunnel filling process if no endless bands are employed. Sticking a 12 inch dowel into the banks of these poles is a practical technique to separate 25% poles from one another. Because it is in touch with moisture, temperature variations, and ammonium residues, the metal sheet that runs through the inside of the door is composed of stainless steel. Two windows are placed on the outside of the composting patio, on the side of the composting patio, that act as a pressure leak of air and steam injected; these vents can be 18x18. They should be the type of eyelashes that only open when positive pressure is applied. An anti-virus or anti-aphid mesh must be placed within the tunnel vents to prevent insects from entering. This form of mesh has too small holes and is more effective than a mosquito net.

System of Ventilation

The density of the compost is taken into account when calculating the capacity of the fan for any tunnel, which ranges from 250 to 300 kg/mt3 when using machines and 180 to 200 kg/mt3 when using manual labor. Consider the following scenario: If you have a tunnel that is 10.00 meters long by 3.00 meters wide and is filled to a height of 1.80 meters with an average weight of 300 kilograms per mt3, the following formula is used: 10.00 x 3.00 x 1.80 = 54 mt3, then 54 mt3 x 300 kg = 16,200 kilograms of compost. The appropriate air ratio for this type of work has been found to be 200 mt3 / hour/ton. With a centrifugal fan and a pressure of 110 cubic millimeters in the water column, a fan that injects 3,240 mt3 of air per hour is required, resulting in a weight of 200 mt3 x 16.2 ton. Composting It is critical to examine the water column pressure since there were issues in testing with fans with 80 and 90 mm pressure due to a lack of air penetration in the compost, and the pasteurization process was not completed in these places.

THE TUNNEL IS BEING FILLED

This maneuver entails placing compost in the tunnel, and the time and quality required to complete it are determined by numerous factors: a) The use of machinery; b) The type of machinery; and c) Operator coordination. Filling the tunnel can be done manually or mechanically, but whatever method is used, it is necessary for the crew to have the necessary equipment and work tools for this and all other operations. The ideal approach to fill the tunnel in every way is to employ endless belts, which will save time, enhance compost aeration, and result in greater compost quality and less physical wear on the workers. A barrier that supports and keeps the fertilizer must be placed at the start of the tunnel filling. A wooden fence can be built to the requisite height of 2.00 mt. - 2.10 mt. by stacking boards on top of each other. The boards are inserted into a PTR, which is a sort of metal rail installed or riveted into the wall. This protects the metal doors from coming into direct touch with the compost and corroding or oxidizing, as well as the entrances from expiring and not closing properly as a result of the instant load. It's also critical that the compote is leveled when filling the tunnel so that there are no lumps on the surface, because the pressure of the injected air is lower in these spots, which might serve as a haven for pests or diseases. Proposal Analyzing both systems reveals that psilocybin mushroom production has remained marginal, owing to a scarcity of competent technicians in the fungal business. The quantity of investment is more than in rural areas, but not to the extent that it is inaccessible to serious investors, but rather because of the lack of alternative structured production plans. That is, a single investor's investment in a production plant is more significant, and even more so if it is built from the ground up and covers all processes; however, if the production processes can be divided into a scheme in which only the work is done until the sowing phase, and the bags are sold to producers who have facilities where the cultivation work is continued, the costs are significantly reduced. The "APIADE" proposal, or "Use of Disused Agricultural Facilities for the Production of Edible

Fungi," is unquestionably an alternative that promises to add value to idle infrastructure and revalue it in such a way that a production structure can be created in which a MATRIX company and SATELLITE producers work together in such a way that the parent company invests in the fermentation facilities. Pasteurization and planting phases are completed so that satellite producers can receive bags for which they have simply spent in the adaptation of their facilities. Previous training sessions in equipment management and cultivation activities, as well as advise on the demands and calculations of satellite producers' facilities for optimal psilocybin mushroom production, would be organized to achieve this. In terms of commercialization, it may go through the parent firm, which would be the sole distributor and seller of the finished product.

Use a Cultivation Procedure That Is Required

Which Mushrooms Do You Want to Grow? Oyster mushrooms, mushrooms, and shiitake mushrooms are the three most basic types for home production. Although the cultivation procedure is similar in all three cases, the appropriate growth media varies. Oyster mushrooms thrive in straw soil or coffee beans (explained further below); shiitake mushrooms thrive in sawdust; and mushrooms thrive in composted manure. The nutritional requirements of each of these species are reflected in their various modes of growth. Each of them, however, can be cultivated in straw or sawdust. If you choose with the latter, be sure the wood isn't treated. The type of fungus you cultivate is entirely up to you. The concept is to cultivate the ones you enjoy the most.

Purchase Psilocybin Mushroom Mycelium that has been prepared.

Mycelia are fungi's root structures, and they can be found in sawdust. They're employed in the same way that plant shoots are to make cultivation easier. You may find high-quality psilocybin mushroom mycelia in a variety of internet sites, garden supply stores, and businesses that specialize in organic products. Make sure you're buying mycelia rather than spores. Spores, which are more comparable to plant seeds, are also sold in some retailers (instead of sprouts). Growing mushrooms from spores takes more time and practice, thus it is best left to more experienced farmers.

CHAPTER FIVE
COFFEE BEANS WITH PSILOCYBIN MUSHROOMS

Purchase Coffee Beans

This is a fun DIY that allows you to reuse the coffee residue from a coffee machine that would otherwise be thrown. Because coffee is sterilized after preparation and is full of nutrients, the leftovers of ground coffee make an excellent culture media for fungi (particularly oyster mushrooms). You'll need 2.5 kg (88 ounces) of traces of fresh coffee to make 500 g (18 ounces) of fungal mycelia. The best technique to obtain this amount is to go to a cafeteria and politely request the remaining coffee from that day's preparation. Most of the time, they are given out without a hitch.

Obtain a Mushroom-Growing Bowl

Obtain a Mushroom-Growing Bowl A culture bag with gauze, which you can get at the same store as the mycelia, is the perfect item for this. If you can't find it, cut four holes on the edges of a large freezer bag or a clean milk carton. Place the Mycelia in the Container and close the lid. Wash your hands thoroughly with bactericidal soap, then use your fingers to combine the fungal mycelia with the coffee residue, making sure to spread them equally. Place the inoculated coffee remnants in a plastic bag or container and lock it tightly. Place the Mushrooms in the Correct Environment Spot the container in a cool, dark place with adequate ventilation, such as a pantry or under the sink, at a temperature of 18 to 25 ° C (65 to 75 ° F). Allow about three weeks for the bag to get totally white (this is because the mycelia begin to colonize the remains of coffee). Remove any dark green or brown bits that emerge on the colonized substrate once more, as they may make you sick. Mushrooms must be relocated. Once the contents of the container have turned completely white, place it somewhere bright but out of direct sunlight, and drill a five-by-five-centimeter (2-by-2-inch) hole in the top. Because fungi do not develop in a dry environment, moisten the contents of the container with water twice a day to keep it from drying out. Mushrooms should be harvested. During the next 5 to 7 days, you'll notice the fungi start to appear. Continue to wet the container, and it will double in size every day. It's time to harvest the hats when they start to lean a little. When the fungus have stopped emerging, put the coffee grounds in your garden with a little compost or compost, and you'll see that fresh mushrooms appear after a while, depending on the weather.

Alternative Culture Procedures should be used

Use a ready-to-grow mushroom package. This strategy might be more simple and enjoyable for individuals with no prior experience. A plastic bag with straw or inoculated and sterilized leaf litter is included in these kits. To grow mushrooms at home, all you have to do is keep the bag in the appropriate circumstances for 7 to 10 days. Most mushroom kinds, such as mushrooms, Crimini, Portobello, lion's head mushrooms, shiitake, and oyster mushrooms, can be utilized using ready-to-use packets that cost between $20 and $30. Open the bag and place it in a bright, but not direct sunlight, location to begin the growing process (as on the inside ledge of a window). The package can be kept at room temperature, but it must be sprayed with water on a daily basis to maintain a high humidity level. Some kits include a plastic bag cover to keep moisture levels in check. After a week or ten days, fungus begin to appear, but you'll likely have two or three more rounds of fungi in a period of one to three months. The nicest part about these packets is that you may bury them in the garden or compost them once you've used them to grow mushrooms. Fungi can then grow back there depending on the weather.

On a Log, Grow Psilocybin Mushrooms

Some fungal species, such as reishi, maitake, lion's mane, shiitake, pearl, and Phoenix oyster mushrooms, can also be grown from a trunk. Inoculating hardwood logs with birch lozenges already infested with fungal mycelia achieves this.

These tablets can be found online or in establishments that specialize in psilocybin mushroom growing. The first step is to locate a good trunk for mushroom cultivation. A hard, non-aromatic timber, such as maple, oak, elm, or poplar, should be used. It must be 1 or 1.5 meters (3 or 4 feet) long with a diameter of no more than 35 cm (14 inches). To allow the tree's inherent fungicidal capabilities to diminish, remove the trunk at least two weeks before planting the crop. You'll need about 50 tablets to colonize a log using these methods. Drill 2 cm (2 cm) deep holes in the log with an 8 mm (5/16 inch) drill bit, following the diamond shape. The holes should be spaced 10 cm (4 inches) apart. Place the birch tablets in the gaps and tap them down firmly with a hammer. If you plan to leave the logs outside, fill the holes with cheese or beeswax to keep the tablets safe from insects and the elements. It is not necessary to seal the holes if they will be stored indoors, in the garage, or in the basement. Fungal mycelia impregnate the trunk over time, colonizing the wood completely. Fungi begin to develop between the cracks in the trunk when this happens. This normally takes 9 to 12 months, but depending on the humidity and temperature conditions, they are likely to emerge every year.

Planting Process in a Nutshell

The optimal temperature for growing these fungi is between 12 and 14 degrees Celsius, with a humidity level of 75 to 80 percent. Even so, they can grow in temperatures ranging from 8 to 18 degrees Celsius without difficulty. From chilly to medium, that is. The first thing to know about this product is that the CO_2 level of the environment plays a critical function during the cultivation process. This should not be more than 0.1 percent, which is why good environmental aeration is critical. Fungi, unlike other crops, lack chlorophyll and hence cannot feed on mineral compounds in the soil. As a result, they must grow on a substrate, which can be manure, to meet their nutritional requirements. Several parameters must be considered for optimum development: nutrients, temperatures, humidity, carbon dioxide, and so on. Planting takes happen in dark, chilly environments such as caves, cellars, mines, and tunnels. You can grow your specimens in individual bags made for this purpose, which are great for beginners, or in wooden trays filled with substrate that are 6 inches deep. When the temperature of the compost reaches 23 - 24° C, use a plastic syringe to inject the mycelia (a mass of hyphae that comprises a fungus' vegetative structure) into the substrate. To stimulate the growth of mycelium and white roots, the substrate must be kept warm for two weeks. A temperature of 21° C is ideal for using an electric pad. Remove the cushioning once the roots have developed because the substrate temperature should be cool from now on. Cover with a layer of earth or moss and cover with a thin towel for about ten days. The revocation prevents the fungus' mycelium from developing and forcing it to bear fruit. Finally, remove the layer and keep moistening the soil twice a day until you see the first mushroom sprouts.

Diseases and Plagues

As previously said, excessive moisture damages the psilocybin mushroom, resulting in the production of molds that are difficult to eradicate with fungicides; the only way to avoid this problem is to prevent it. It's a good idea to sanitize the drawers after each harvest before using them again. When it comes to producing psilocybin mushrooms in your home garden, you should be aware that the most common pests include mites, nematodes, and a variety of insects:

PSEUDOMONAS TOLAASII, PSEUDOMONAS TOLAASII, PSEUDOMONAS TOLA

• MOLD IN THE COLOR OF GREEN

• BACTERIAL GLUE OR SPOT

• DISEASE OF THE DRY BLADDER

• BUBBLE, DRY OR MOLE

MYCOGEN is a protein that is produced by my body.

• FRAUDULENT TRUFFLE

•MUMMIFICATION MUMMIFICATION MUMMIFICATION MU

VIRUSES ARE

DIPTERAL DISEASE

Pests

• SPIDER RED

• SPIDER BLONDE

THE THE WHITE SPIDER

• COBWEB MOLD, FABRIC

• NEMATODES are parasitic worms.

•BEETLES

PSEUDOMONAS TOLAASII is a kind of PSEUDOMONAS.

• Habitat: They can be found in large numbers in many types of aquatic soils and ecosystems. They multiply on mushrooms that have been kept damp for an extended period of time. • Water, various forms of covering, compost, flies, mites, nematodes, tools, and workers are the most common methods of multiplication. • Macroscopic appearance: Yellowish spots or circles on mushrooms, irregular lesions They multiply quickly in moist mushrooms, turn brown, and then slug; they also have an awful odor.

MOLD, GREEN

• Habitat: It's found in a lot of compost and on a lot of things. Many species can be found growing on wood and other plant tissue.

• Propagation method: It is mostly an air contaminant, but it is also found in soils. During harvest and irrigation, it spreads. He enjoys being in an acidic environment. When found in the compost, it indicates that the fermentation, pasteurization, and conditioning processes were not completed effectively, and that the compost is not selective enough.

• Microscopically, a cottony mold that forms circular colonies on the compost or cover. It starts out gray, but as it grows, it turns green due to the generation of spores. Brown patches on the hat of parasitized fungi are comparable to those of verticillium. Trichoderma thrives in compost that has a lot of available carbohydrates and isn't supplemented with enough nitrogen, as well as when the cover material has a lot of plant debris. Trichoderma harzianum has recently been linked to one of the world's most serious mushroom-growing illnesses. This species is being utilized to manage fungal infections in flower and vegetable crops in our country, resulting in an active spore load in the environment.

GLUE OR BACTERIAL SPOT

This results in yellow dots on the hat that are sticky and appear as drops. There were recognized in groups and races, each of which has a particular pathogenicity for Chile. It's also worth noting that additional bacterial spot-causing species have been proposed, including X. vesicatoria, X. perforator, X. Gardner, and X. euvesicatoria.

The onset of illness

Because of its near to the sea, Sinaloa provides a great setting for its development, with a hot climate and high relative humidity. Temperatures between 20-35°C during the day and night, with humidity of 75-80%, enhance the spread of the disease. Infection is further exacerbated by the presence of hot and rainy periods, particularly if drops of water are deposited on the leaves and infection develops during the crop's earliest phenological stages. As a result of the favorable climatic circumstances for bacterial staining, this disease can substantially impair the plant health of vegetables grown in greenhouses, such as tomatoes or mushrooms, due to the high planting densities used. The bacterium enters the plant through natural openings like stomata and wounds created by a variety of factors (insects, wind, workers). It wouldn't be able to penetrate the plant on its own. Its subsequent dispersal is accomplished through irrigation, water splashes, and social work. X.vesicatoria can only survive in the soil for long periods of time if it feeds on plant wastes that serve as host plants. It can also be found in infected fruits, transplants, weeds, and cultivated species' seeds. Bacterial spot is a disease that affects tomato and mushroom cultivation in the state of Sinaloa, causing major production losses and thus being classified as a limiting factor. It's found all throughout the world, although it's most common in tropical and subtropical areas, where excessive rainfall affects Solanaceae at any phenological stage. X. campestris PV. vesicatoria was thought to be the causal agent of this bacterial disease at first. Following that, three pathogenic groupings were discovered: 1) A pathogen in tomato culture, 2) a pathogen in mushroom culture, and 3) a pathogen in both tomato and mushroom cultures. There were recognized in groups and races, each of which has a particular pathogenicity for Chile. It's also worth noting that additional bacterial spot-causing species have been proposed, including X. vesicatoria, X. perforator, X. Gardner, and X. euvesicatoria.

Symptom

About a week after the plant is infected, symptoms appear in both seedlings and adult plants. Depending on the temperature, this time can last anywhere from 5 to 15 days. At temperatures above 20 ° C, the sickness progresses more quickly. Symptoms in the foliage include: Both the leaf limbus and the leaf petiole show symptoms. The lesions are initially round and fluid (pustules), with a yellowish halo surrounding them in the majority of instances. The lesions expand, lose their spherical shape, and the center of the wound darkens as it becomes dehydrated and finally fractures as the infection progresses. The infection level in young leaves is higher than in the remainder of the leaves. The disease produces more serious damage at the leaf level than in the stem for the same reason: the lignin content of plant tissues. As a result, bacterial spots on chili seedlings can cause significant defoliation (leaf deformation) that has a negative impact on the farm's overall performance. Symptoms in the stem: Pustules in the stem resemble those seen in the leaves and fruits, but they are darker and bulkier. Symptoms in fruits: The disease's lesions can be noticed on the fruit's epidermis (quality loss), as well as on the peduncle and calyx. The fruits frequently develop abnormally when the virus affects the peduncle. Other diseases, either cryptogamic or not, can develop around the sores caused by the bacterium.

Controlling Bacterial Stains

Controlling the situation in advance Healthy seed, ideally certified, should be used. If necessary, treat it as follows: 1) Heat treatment: Soak the seeds in 50°C water for 25 minutes, then drain and dry. This therapy is not suggested for chili seeds. 2) Bactericidal/fungicidal treatment: Soak the seeds for one minute in a 1.3 percent sodium hypochlorite solution, rinse, and dry. 3) Opt for tolerant or resistant varieties. There is no sort of bacteria that is impervious to all strains. 4) Proper greenhouse ventilation is essential. Reduce the temperature by using methods that do so. 5) Do not perform social work while the plants are damp. 6) Crop rotation: By rotating crops, the inoculum load for the next crop can be significantly reduced. Solanaceae are not recommended for rotation since they are X. vesicatoria host plants. 7) Get rid of any plants that show signs of the disease. After that, they should be put in plastic bags and taken out of the greenhouse. 8) To get rid of surplus moisture, use full planting frames with plenty of ventilation. 9) Ensure proper management of sprayed treatments and calculate an adequate supply and frequency of watering to avoid excessive humidity. Sprinkler irrigation should be avoided. 10) Remove weeds, diseased plants, and crop/crop remains (particularly those belonging to the Solanaceae family). 11) Maintaining good hygiene. Work tools should be disinfected on a regular basis because they are a major source of disease transmission. 12) Maintain ideal nutritional conditions for the crop. Avoid nitrogen-rich diet since it makes plant tissue more sensitive to diseases such as bacterial spot; this makes the plant physiologically stronger against possible diseases. Control using chemicals This disease's chemical control is difficult. Because there are so many species and races, resistance to the active compounds utilized is likely to emerge quickly. As a result, regular copper-based therapies are indicated to avoid the condition. Once the pathogen has been established in the crop, you might opt to apply two weekly copper treatments and alternatively apply Mancozeb and Maneb in one of them to strengthen copper's fungicidal and bactericidal functions and prevent resistance. Control of biological processes The use of bacteriophages to reduce illness in transplants has proven a success at the seedbed level. DISEASE OF THE DRY BLADDER Because the spores spread swiftly, dry bladder illness can cause a variety of issues. To avoid the spread of the disease across your nursery, it's critical to detect and remove the first afflicted fungi. How do you get rid of the initial fungus infection? Dry bladder disease is spread via spores. The spores are sticky and spread from everything that can adhere to them, such as B. people, flies, dust, and water. Covering and removing an infected fungus is the greatest approach to prevent spores from spreading. Using a disinfectant such as alcohol or alcohol, moisten a handkerchief. A moist cloth attracts the spores. Slowly and carefully Place the damp handkerchief over the diseased fungus without producing turbulence, which could cause spores to fly away. Clothe your palm with a synthetic bag and draw the truffle upward with the proper amount of the surrounding ground while closing the truffle with the paper handkerchief. Close the envelope and turn the bag with the infected fungus over. After steaming the growing chamber, leave the bag of infected mushroom in the growth room and discard it. There are various methods you can use, such as using a plastic bottle. Remove the container's bottom, set the bottle over the infected fungus, and fill with salt. Make sure you don't spread the spores, no matter what method you utilize. A single drop of water on an infected fungus would spread billions of spores rather than scatter them - a single droplet of water on an infected fungus would be less than a meter away from the fungus would spread billions of spores. A few days later, several mushrooms around this original mushroom began to display the first signs of a bladder disease. In the coming days, check the field where you isolated the sick fungus to determine if the disease has returned.

BUBBLE, DRY OR MOLE

• Habitat: It is a common mushroom parasite. During harvest, excessive humidity mixed with poor air circulation promotes the growth of Verticillium. It grows in a wide variety of temperatures, but prefers temperatures over 17 ° C. Soils are rich in Verticillium.

• Mode of transmission: Harvesters, flies, other insects, and rodents are the main carriers of the disease from a contaminated to a healthy environment. More spores were distributed when infected fungus were irrigated.

• Macroscopic appearance: Slightly infected mushrooms have brown spots on their hats, which eventually turn into a grey veil as spores develop. Sectioned stems and twisted fungus are visible when the infection is earlier. Spores are also transmitted by air, using filthy machinery. It produces deformations and eventually causes the mushroom to decompose. The predominant mushroom mycoparasite grown in the region of La Manchuela in the provinces of Cuenca and Albacete is Verticillium fungicola, also known as Mole Seca. The value of dry Mole (Verticillium fungicola) suffering is primarily attributable to:

• The disease's difficulty in eradication • The ease with which it circulates

• The fungicides' ineffectiveness, which is likely linked to the emergence of resistant strains Verticillium fungicola - Verticillium fungicola - Verticillium fungicola - Verticillium fungicola - Verticillium fungi The illness's resurgence, as well as the financial consequences, demonstrate the importance and severity of the "dry mole" in mushroom production, indicating that Verticillium fungicola disease remains a financial menace to mushroom growers in Castilla-La Stain. It also follows from the study that ineffectual control methods must be sustained, among which we advise, like GANDY (1981), the idea of finishing the crop quickly, a practice that may be of ultimate importance for the explosion's hygiene. WONG and PREECE (1987) corroborate this proposal by pointing out the increase in a load of dry mole spores as crop age grows, implying that the advent of Verticillium in the fourth florade was a substantial contributor to the total loss of the harvest in Pennsylvania mushroom farms. In summary, the strength of the Mushroom Verticillium fungicola dry Mole disease grows as the blooms mature, indicating an accumulation of infectious inoculum. On the other hand, there is a hint of the necessity for "in vitro" fungicide tests to rule out the creation of prochloraz-resistant V. fungicla strains. Technicians that specialize in mushroom production offer advice on how to combat the Dry Mole of the Champion - Verticillium fungicola:

Dry mushroom mole (Verticillium fungicola) is the name of the disease.

• Treatment guidelines: If the presence of contaminated sources in surrounding crops necessitates it.

• Prochloraz (45%) is a well-known active ingredient (46 percent)

• Treatment method: irrigation water

• Treatment time: 7-9 days after the covering is removed.

• Dose: 1 gram of commercial product per m2 of crop area in 1 liter of water.

• Protection period: 8 days (45%) - 2 days (46 percent)

• Toxicology: Dangerous

MYCOGEN

• Other names include bubble, moist bubble, and mole.

• Habitat: Very prevalent, causing major crop losses by infecting mushrooms. It can be found in the soil naturally. It does not thrive in temperatures below 15 degrees Celsius.

• Propagation method: Mostly through inadequately disinfected covering. Workers, as well as dirty work equipment and insects, are important sources of spore dispersal. Irrigation of afflicted sites carried the pollutant even further.

• Macroscopic appearance: It looks as a white mold that has affected the primordium and turned it into a soft white mycelium mass. An amber liquid holding the spores flows from the decaying center of these aggregates.

TRUFFLE WITHOUT PROOF

• Habitat: It thrives in the depths of the compost.

• Propagation method: The spores enter with the compost or the covering material, especially if the compost or covering material is prepared directly on the ground.

• Macroscopic appearance: Gray-white carpophores, which can be mistaken for dead immature mushrooms. They grow in the compost or on the mycelium in the cover.

• Comments: An increased temperature (more than 28 ° C) is required for the false truffle spores to grow. It develops nicely above 16 ° C once germinated.

MUMMIFICATION

• Disease caused by the pseudomonas bacterium Pseudomonas aeruginosa and other unidentified pseudomonas species.

• Habitat: The bacteria was discovered to develop intracellularly within the host.

• Mode of transmission: The disease is propagated by infected mycelium (carried by insects and workers) rather than spores. The virus moves at a 10 to 30 centimeter per day speed.

• Macroscopic appearance: Infected mushrooms have curved stems and bases that are encircled by a crown or overgrowth of mycelium. Dwarf and slanted hats are frequent.

VIRUSES

The habitat of viruses is other particles or organisms, which makes it a tough disease to identify. Infection-infected mushroom spores or infected mycelium are used to propagate the virus. As a result, air, insects, filthy containers and instruments, humans, and poor sanitation conditions exist. The degree to which virosis manifests itself in a crop is determined by the period of infection and the number of sick spores. The following are some symptoms that may present alone or in combination: The first wave arrived later than usual. The shading and stem are practically indistinguishable. Stems were extended and hunched in many cases. Envelopes that have been flattened. The veil forms at a lower level than usual. The fungi varies in color from greyish-white to brown. Mushrooms have a sloppy surface, develop slowly and open fast, and remain too tiny. Bacterial secondary infection causes hats to turn dark brown and rot. They appear to originate beneath the surface of the ground at times, and when they sprout, they are already open. Virus infection is particularly difficult to diagnose and establish. Optical microscopes can't see the virus particles since they're so little. Furthermore, the indications of virosis can be totally undetectable, resulting in performance decreases for no apparent reason.

COBWEB MOLD, FABRIC

• Habitat: Often seen on the mushroom cover or parasitizing it.

• Airborne spores, cover, water, and insects are all methods of propagation.

• Macroscopic appearance: It resembles a spider web, appearing in scattered spots at first and quickly spreading across the cover, engulfing everything in its course.

Pests

• WHITE SPIDER: Cavities in the foot and cap are irregular.

• BLONDE SPIDER: This allows the fungus' roots to spread out.

• RED SPIDER: The workers are irritated by it.

• DIPTERAL: A pest whose larvae ruin the fungus' mycelium, causing fruiting failures and causing damage to the fungi that have already grown.

• BEETLES: The bat develops little oval holes.

• NEMATODES: Destroy the fungus' mycelium.

Care That Is Required Growing mushrooms in your yard at home is difficult, but it is possible with the use of greenhouses with dark covers to aid development. Here are some helpful hints:

• Natural dung, especially from a horse or donkey, is frequently used as the substrate. Because it must be made from wheat or rye straw, it must originate from working animals that do not eat fresh fodder or green food.

• Different species of mushrooms necessitate various substrates.

• The crop should be kept at a consistent temperature of 12-14o C. When the temperature is below 10 degrees Celsius, the harvest is exceedingly slow. When the temperature rises above 18 degrees Celsius, the fungus distort, and infections become more prevalent.

• Hone your talents and take the risk of growing mushrooms. During the process, you will learn a lot and your palette will be delighted.

Harvest

Many people are drawn out into the forest during mushroom season to satisfy their appetite. If a few basic rules of etiquette are followed, the pleasure of picking wonderful mushrooms and later converting them into delectable recipes will not be impaired.

Conservation of the environment

In late summer and autumn, the psilocybin mushroom season returns. After that, many people go out into the forests and fields to fulfill their passion for food. If a few things are observed, the thrill of hunting for tasty mushrooms, discovering them, and afterwards converting them into exquisite recipes stays unaffected: Fungi can be found in a wide range of biotopes. Access to nature reserves and national parks is subject to restrictions. Chanterelles, porcini mushrooms, and chestnuts are all well-known forest mushrooms. Among the spruce and pine trees, chestnuts are prized. In both deciduous and coniferous forests, porcini and chanterelles mushrooms can be found. The well-known meadow mushroom thrives in pastures and meadows. If the sites have been over-fertilized, however, mushrooms should not be harvested if they still grow. It's worth looking for mushrooms like blood-red boletus or pearl mushroom in parks that haven't been sprayed with pesticides. Delicious mushrooms, such as the parasol, can even be found growing alongside busy streets. However, because the mushrooms are badly diseased, it is not recommended that you eat them.

How Do You Gather Psilocybin Mushrooms?

Every psilocybin mushroom collector needs an excellent descriptive book. Mushroom tours, such as those offered by adult education centers, are advised for newcomers. If you're going "into the mushrooms," there are a few things you should keep in mind:

• Only gather what you know or can 100% determine.

• There's a chance that some edible mushrooms will be confused with toadstools that appear similar.

Meadow mushrooms and tuber agarics are two classic examples. A notable distinguishing trait is: Tuberous mushrooms contain white lamellae, while meadow mushrooms have pink or brown lamellae. If you're having trouble identifying mushrooms, it's best to leave them alone or go to a mushroom assistance center (addresses at local authorities or health offices). Collect only as many mushrooms as you need. Too young and too old mushrooms are left on the table. Older mushrooms that have been eaten by maggots or snails should not be destroyed since they still produce spores that are utilized for reproduction. With a small, pointed knife, carefully unscrew the mushrooms or cut them near to the ground. Tear it out instead, as this will harm the underground mushroom network, the mycelium. Fill any holes in the ground with humus or leaves to keep the mushroom network from drying out. Clean the mushrooms when you find them and transport them in an airtight basket. Mushrooms have a modest nutritional value, yet their vitamin and mineral richness rivals that of many vegetables. They should be kept cool and dry for 24 hours before eating. Raw mushrooms should not be eaten since they can be indigestible or even poisonous. Furthermore, most fungi only develop their distinct scent when properly processed (roast, braise, grill, stew.). Because mushrooms are difficult to digest, mushroom dishes should not be overly expensive and should not be consumed late in the evening. Poisoning is suspected if symptoms such as sweating, diarrhea, or drowsiness arise after eating mushrooms. Consult a doctor or clinic as soon as possible. Poison control centers can also be found in major cities such as Berlin, Hamburg, and Munich. If you ate less than five hours ago, you'll need to vomit to empty your stomach (tickling the palate). Take the vomit and leftovers to the doctor to have the poisons identified. If the poisoning is only discovered after eight hours or longer, call an emergency doctor right away since there is a serious risk of death that can be avoided if a few basic rules of conduct are followed. When is the Best Time to Harvest?

The mushroom should be harvested before it produces spores if you wish to eat it. Before the velum starts to rip or the hat "bends up," depending on the mushroom kind. The velum is the fragile skin on the mushroom hat's root that protects the mushroom's lamella. Oyster mushrooms, for example, should be taken as soon as possible since they get woody as they age. If you want to make a spore print, wait until the hat is completely unfolded. When you're collecting the mushrooms, make sure you turn them out completely. Under no circumstances should the remaining portion of the stem be cut off, since this could cause the substrate to decay and get infected. If a little hole remains, cover it with some vermiculite or covering dirt. Supposed "aborts" must be eradicated. Aborts are miniature fruiting bodies that haven't fully grown. These, too, can begin to deteriorate. It's time to collect the pinheads when they've grown into full-sized mushrooms. When the fungus's foot becomes a little soft and the entire mushroom becomes softer to the touch, it's ripe. It's critical to collect them before the tissue covering the hymenium breaks. They must be carefully removed so as not to harm the crop. What is your opinion on the method? To twist the hat, carefully grasp it between your fingers and twist it. To avoid creating rot pockets, avoid cutting them. It's best to eat them when they're fresh because that's when they'll taste the best. Another alternative is to dry them out and use them later.

Gathering Food from the Wild

You may help fungi thrive and survive in the forest by following a few simple principles when harvesting mushrooms. In addition, having the right equipment allows for more natural processing in the kitchen. It will soon be time to harvest if the first fruiting bodies appear on the tree trunks. When the edges of the mushroom hats tear and protrude upwards, or the spores that have already fallen off congregate on the wood, the fruiting bodies should travel into the kitchen. To do so, twist the mushrooms off with a small movement or chop them off with a sharp knife on the stem. Nothing stands in the way of you enjoying your garden's culinary delights any longer. Forest inhabitants are added to our cuisine in a variety of forms, including fried, risotto, and fresh.

Equipment is required.

You need bring the following items with you to the forest to collect mushrooms:

• A cotton cloth that is clean and dry

• A kitchen knife with a good edge

• A gentle transport basket Even if you have a book with you to identify the different varieties of mushrooms, there is no substitute for experience and knowledge when it comes to mushroom picking. As a result, only gather mushrooms in the forest and on the meadow whose non-toxicity can be determined with certainty.

Lightly separate the mushrooms from the earth.

There are numerous points of view on how to properly harvest mushrooms. While some mushroom pickers cut the mushroom stem near the soil with a sharpened knife, other collectors condemn this approach. Germs should be able to penetrate the fungal mycelium in this fashion, and the stem base is essential for the identification and separation of poisonous variants in specific types. Turn the mushrooms carefully out of the earth by hand and cover the experimentation area with soil. In some cases, a new fungal fruiting body might emerge from the field in the same location in a short period of time.

Preserve the Mushroom's Original Flavor

Harvest only fresh and clean mushrooms, and leave decaying and worm-eaten mushrooms undamaged in the wild. These can be utilized as animal food and their spores can be used to increase the quantity of fungi. Mushrooms are cleaned with a dry towel or a sharp knife if they are found. They should not be cleaned with water before use, since this will cause them to lose their flavor.

How to Make the Most of Your Mushrooms

Fungi as food have a high nutritional percentage that is comparable to the highest-quality animal products, emphasizing their relevance. Is it true that man's nutritional requirements necessitate the consumption of essential amino acids, which are found in only a few foods, rather than the combination of foods required to obtain a balanced diet? 1 cup rice, 1 cup sliced mushroom, 1 onion, 2 garlic cloves, Lenten Chile to taste, Parsley to taste the oil Ingredients: 1 cup rice, 1 cup sliced mushroom, 1 onion, 2 garlic cloves, Lenten Chile to taste, Parsley to taste the oil Prepare the rice by soaking it in boiling water for 15 minutes. It's been drained and rinsed. The grain is then cooked in oil until it is clear and loose. Excess fat is eliminated. Using a cup of water, combine parsley, garlic, and onion. Toss the rice with the sauce and cook for a few minutes. Salt, 3 cups water, mushrooms, and chili are added to the pot. Cover the pot and leave it alone until the rice is tender. 1/2 kilogram mushrooms, 2 medium onions, 2 pasilla peppers, 2 garlic cloves, chicken or beef broth, Epazote, Oil, Salt to taste Ingredients: 1/2 kg mushrooms, 2 medium onions, 2 pasilla peppers, 2 garlic cloves, chicken or beef broth, Epazote, Oil, Salt to taste The onion is chopped into tiny slices before being cooked. Garlic and onion are cooked in a pot until they are translucent. Over low heat, add split or whole mushrooms and cook until they lose their water. Once the broth, roasted pasilla peppers, salt, and epazote have been consumed, pour the remaining broth, roasted pasilla peppers, salt, and epazote. Allow 5 to 10 minutes for them to boil. It's also served.

SEEDING ADVICE

Area for cooling and seeding

The amount of seed is calculated based on the substrate's moist weight. It is suggested that you utilize a grain amount ranging from 3.5 to 5% of the damp substrate's importance (assuming 75 percent humidity). For example, 3.5 to 5 kg of seed is utilized for every 100 kg of wet straw. It's not a good idea to use a lot of seed (more than 5%), because the substrate can get too hot. Because the straw absorbs humidity and maintains the ideal temperature, the bag is filled with a 10 cm substrate layer. Then a layer of seed (which reaches out to receive the hand and disperse it around the bag's periphery), and so on, until the appropriate height is attained, at which point the bag closes neatly.

This is placed in the incubation chamber, tagged with the sowing date. Optimal Development Conditions

Temperature (between 20 and 30 ° C), luminosity (less than 20%), humidity (80 percent relative humidity), and cleansing are all necessary for the mushroom fungus to thrive and flourish efficiently.

What Are the Requirements?

Materials in the Raw Oatmeal bales (two) 5 kg of mycelium Equipment and Materials 1 water drum with a capacity of 200 liters and no lid 1 huge burner or sufficient fuel to heat the drum's water 60x40 cms in 25 bags 2 liters of booze a total of 20 labels a raffia strew of ten meters There are five squirrels in total. a single atomizer

Recommendation at the End

The ideal method for cultivating the psilocybin mushroom depends on the season and location of the intended farmed field. I recommend that you irrigate the mushroom field at least twice a day, and that you remember that psilocybin mushrooms grow best in a cool, shaded environment because they don't require sunshine to process their food, which is why I refer to them as "blind organisms." The psilocybin mushroom is a great way to make money because it's in high demand in the market due to its numerous talents and uses. So I urge that you begin cultivating it, as described in this book, in any region, season (while it is slightly seasonal to produce outstanding products, it can be grown in a comfortable setting to provide excellent results), and time. I wish you good luck with your cultivation and harvesting.

www.ingramcontent.com/pod-product-compliance
Lightning Source LLC
LaVergne TN
LVHW020943030425
807644LV00027B/499